CLASSIC ROCK
FOR *Classical Guitar*

ISBN 978-1-4584-5128-6

HAL•LEONARD®
CORPORATION
7777 W. BLUEMOUND RD. P.O. BOX 13819 MILWAUKEE, WI 53213

Visit Hal Leonard Online at
www.halleonard.com

Behind Blue Eyes

Words and Music by Peter Townshend

Tuning:
(low to high) D-A-D-G-B-E

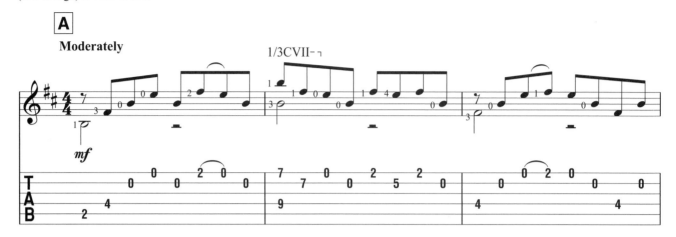

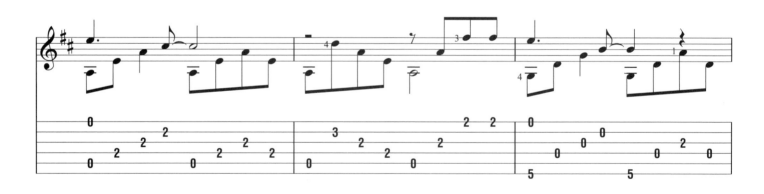

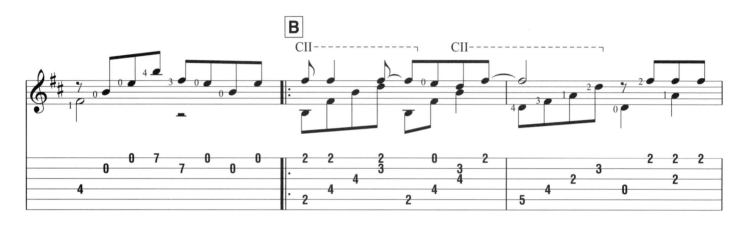

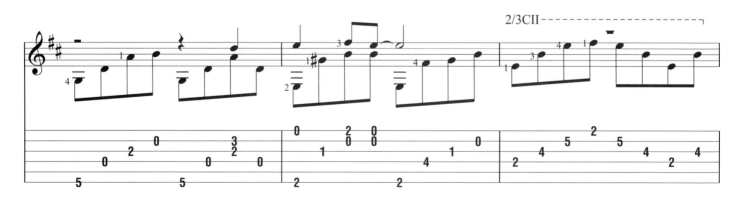

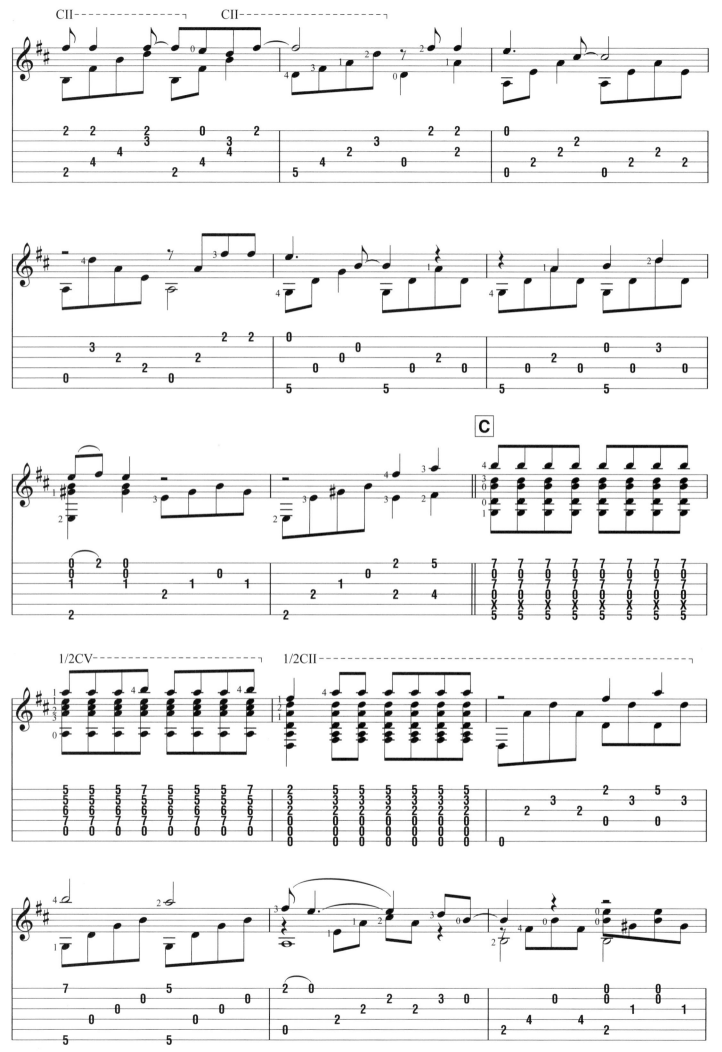

3

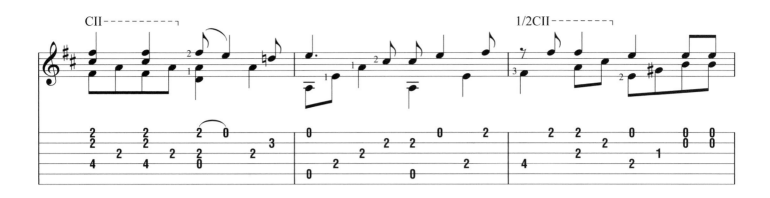

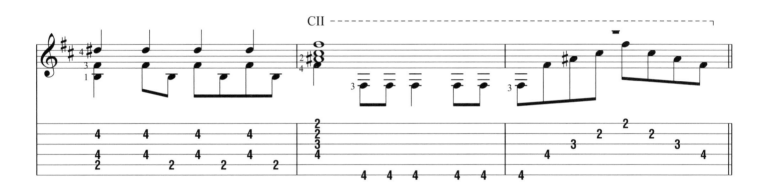

E

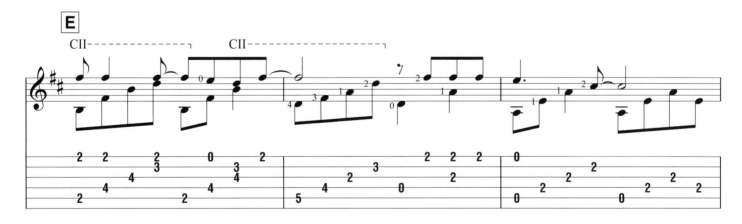

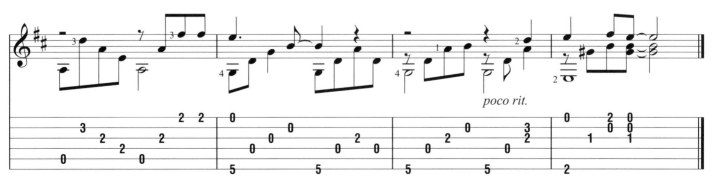

Don't Fear the Reaper

Words and Music by Donald Roeser

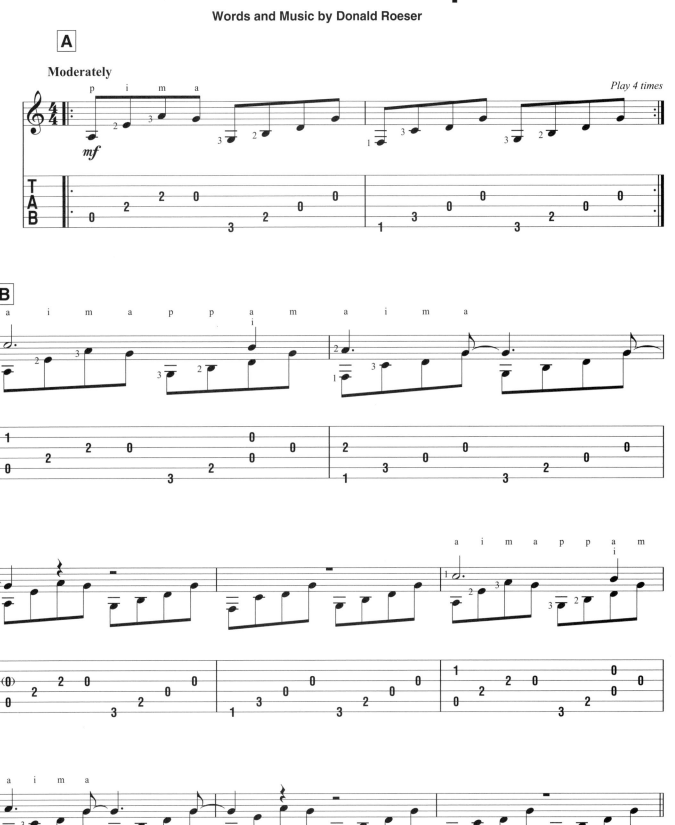

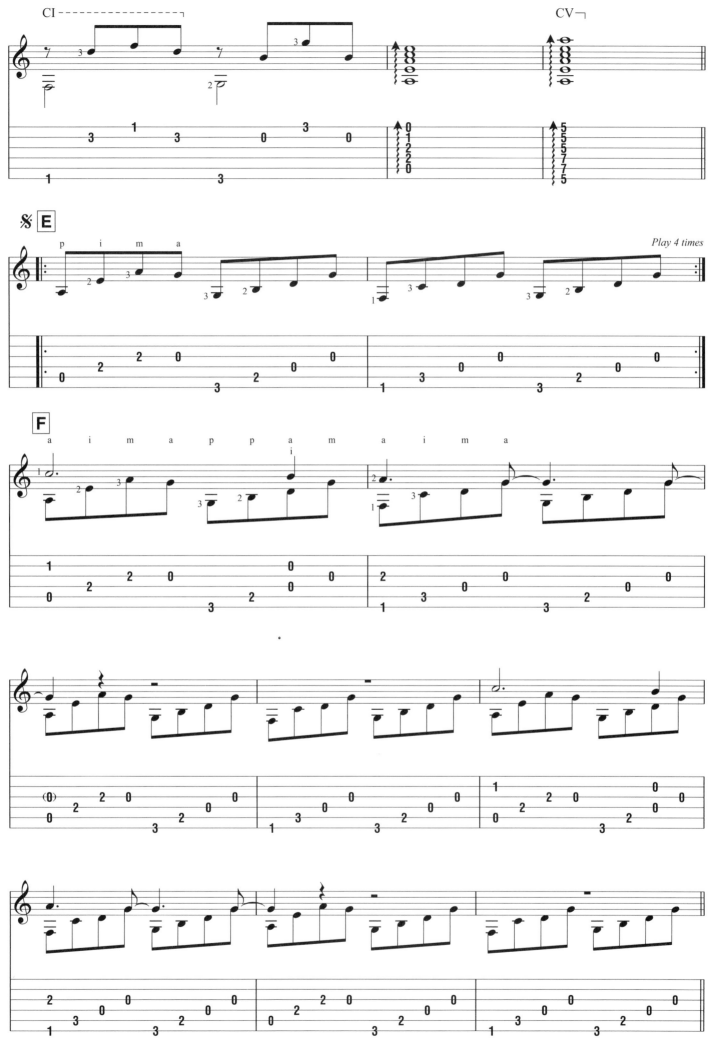

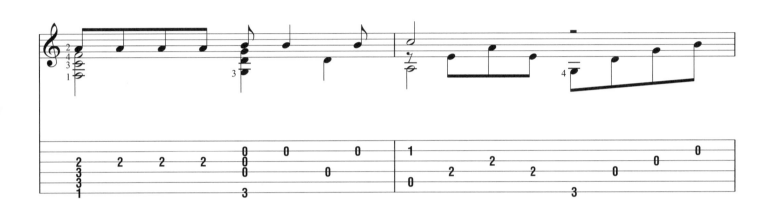

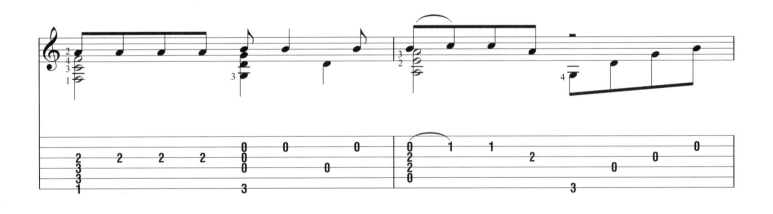

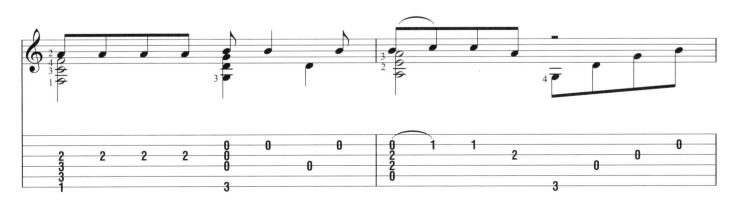

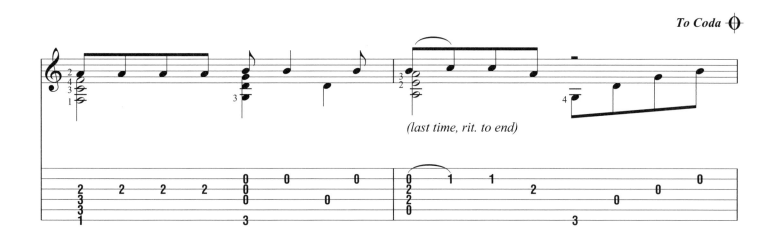

(last time, rit. to end)

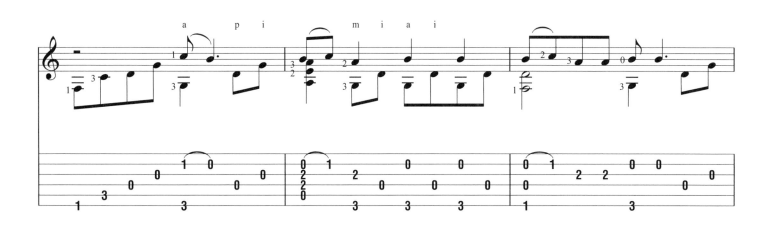

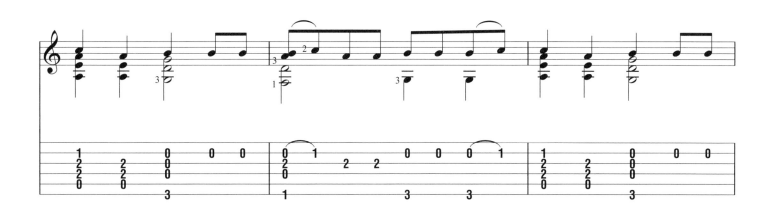

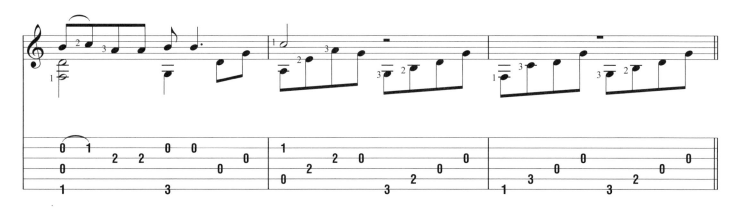

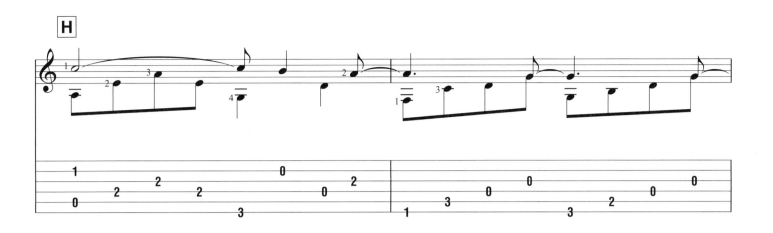

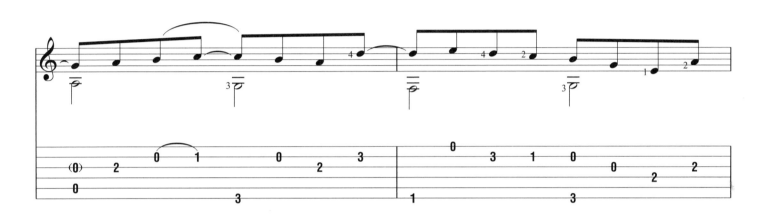

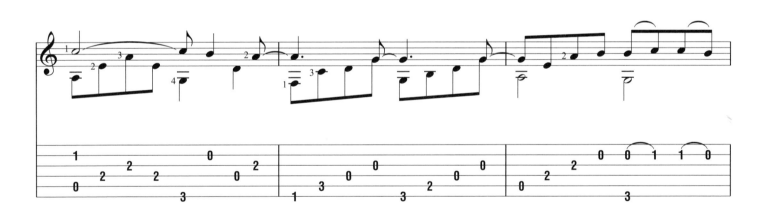

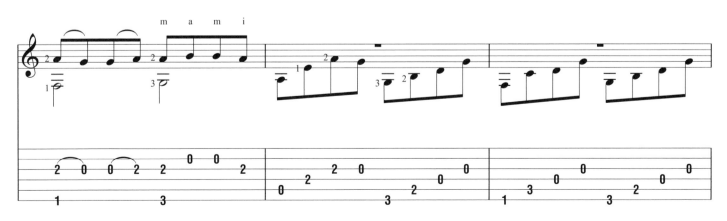

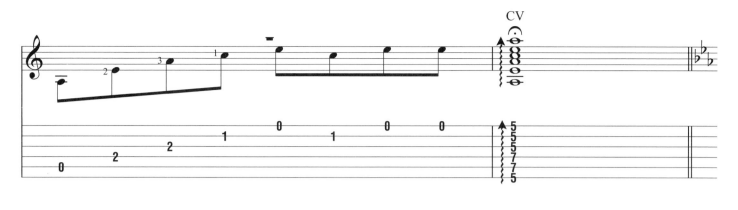

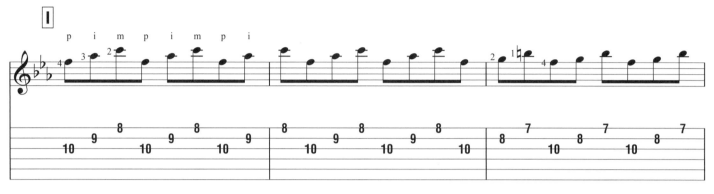

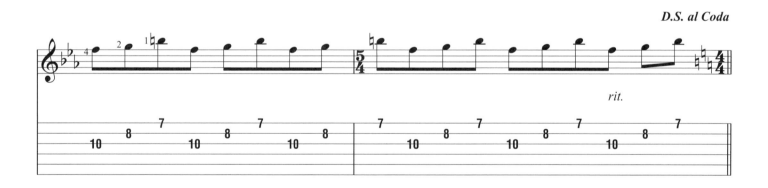

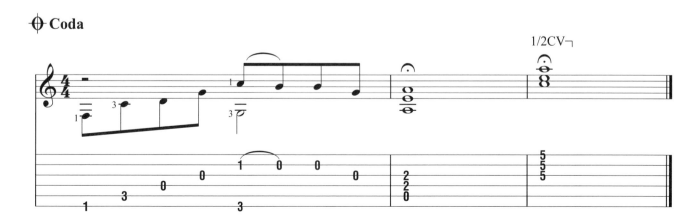

Dust in the Wind

Words and Music by Kerry Livgren

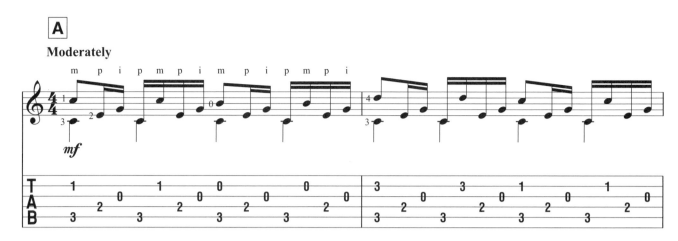

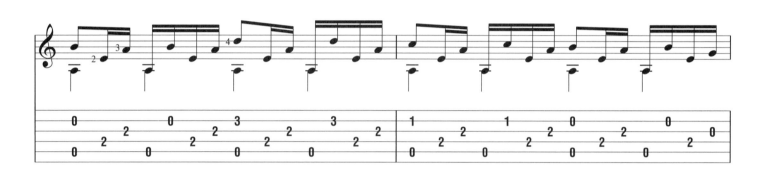

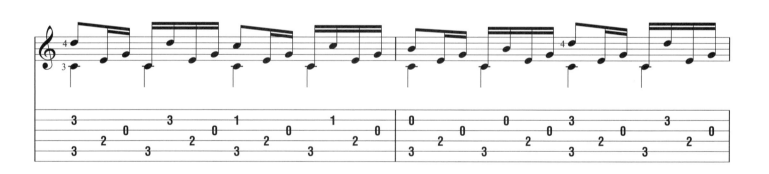

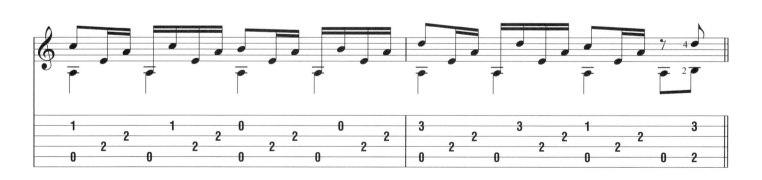

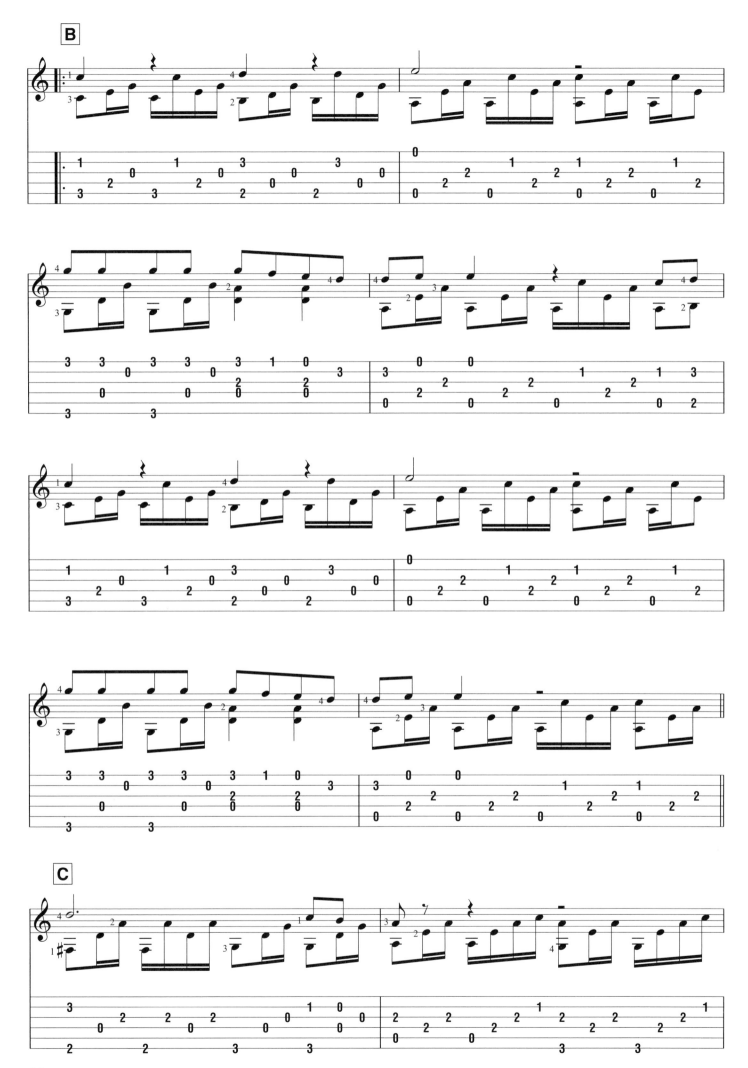

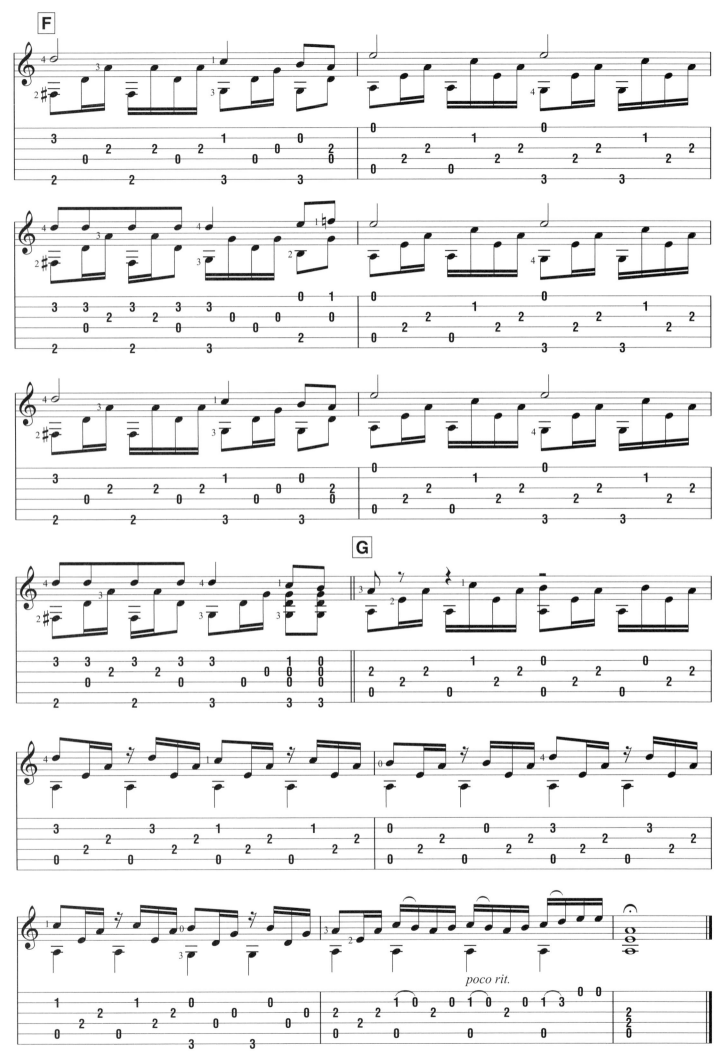

poco rit.

Have You Ever Seen the Rain?

Words and Music by John Fogerty

Tuning:
(low to high) D-A-D-G-B-E

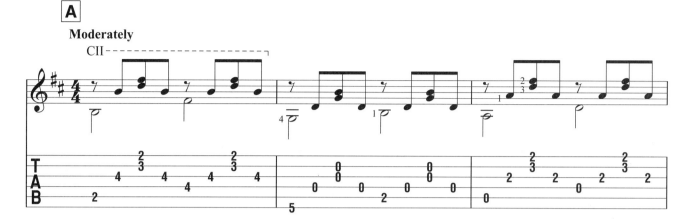

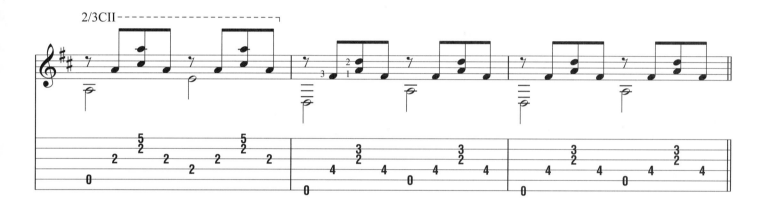

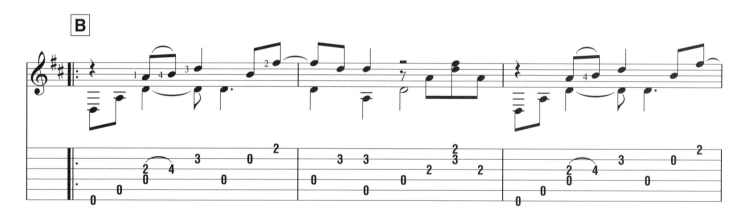

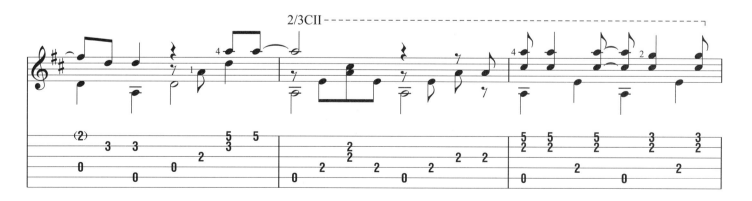

Beth

Words and Music by Bob Ezrin, Stanley Penridge and Peter Criss

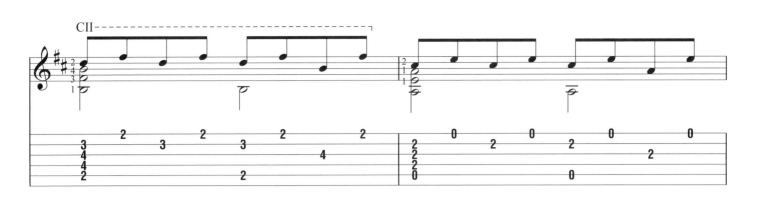

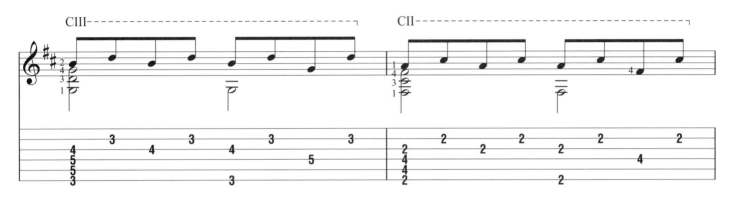

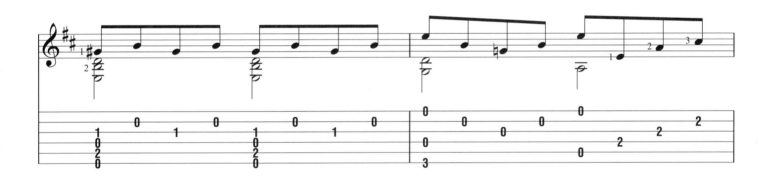

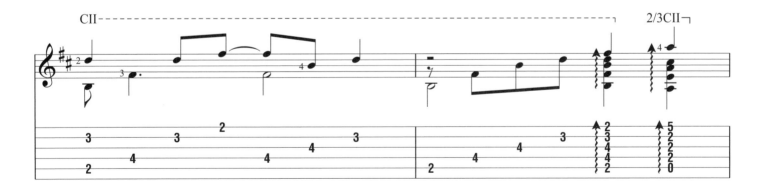

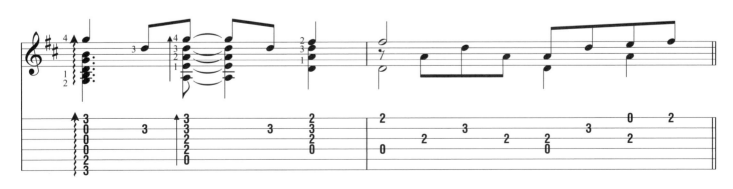

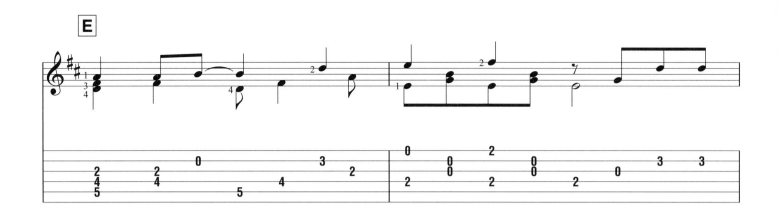

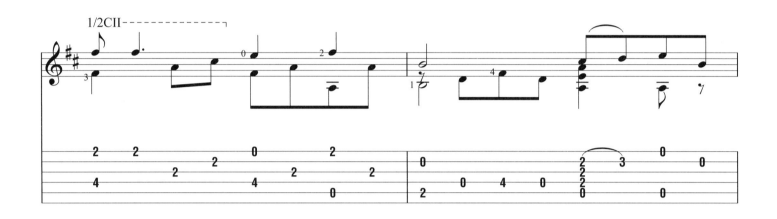

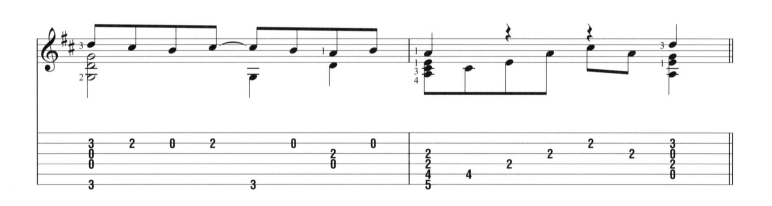

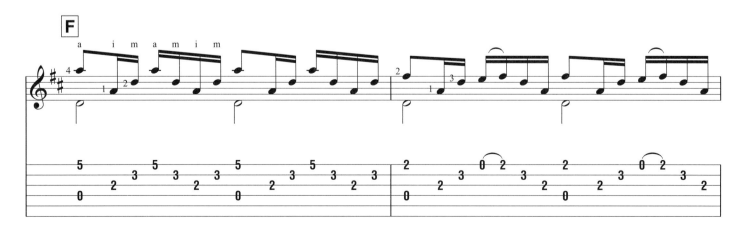

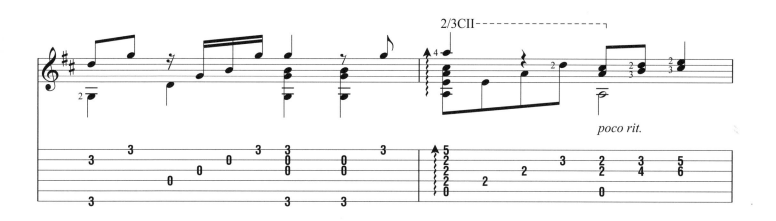

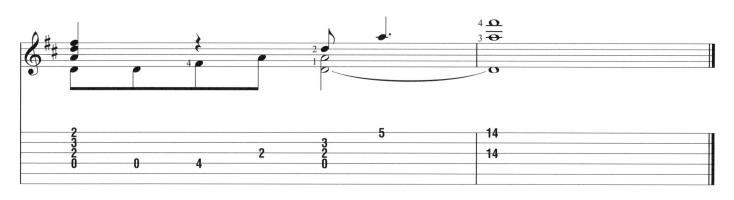

Bohemian Rhapsody

Words and Music by Freddie Mercury

Free Bird

Words and Music by Allen Collins and Ronnie Van Zant

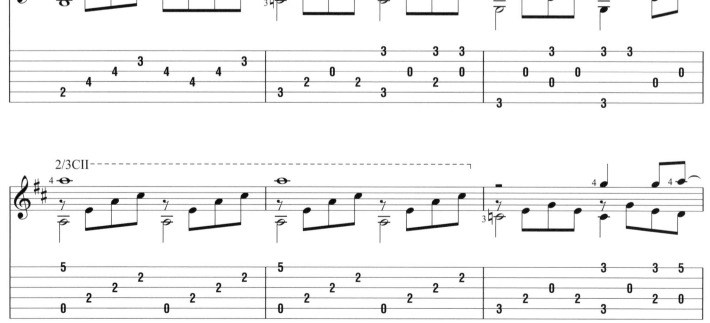

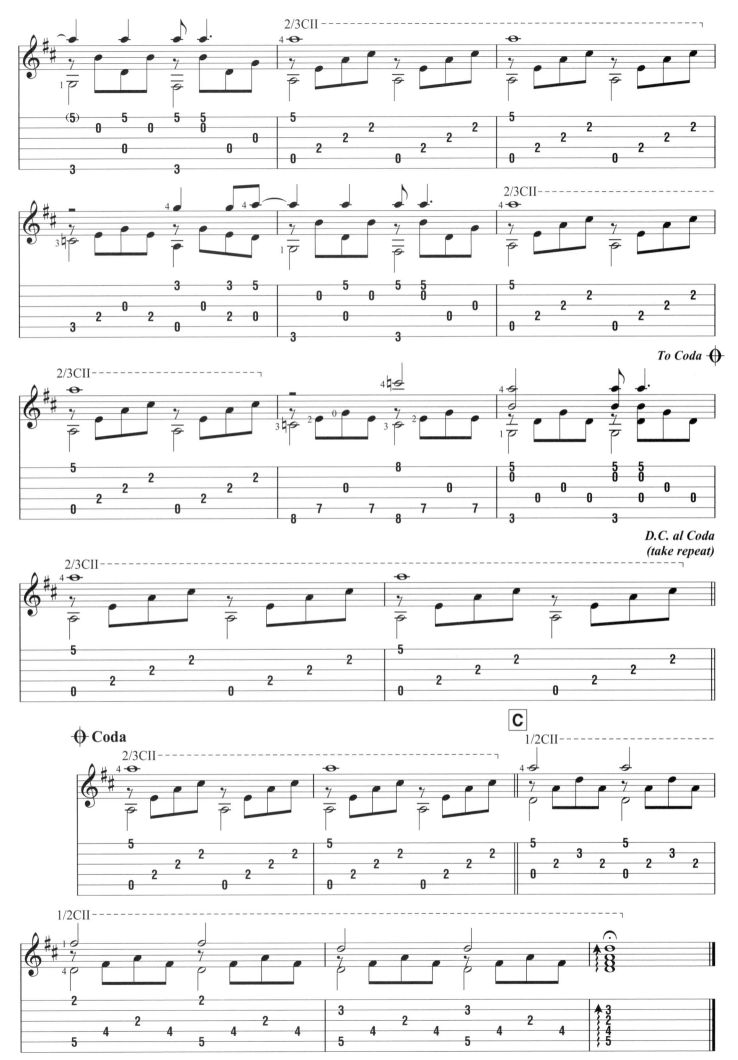

To Coda ⊕

D.C. al Coda
(take repeat)

⊕ Coda

The House of the Rising Sun

Words and Music by Alan Price

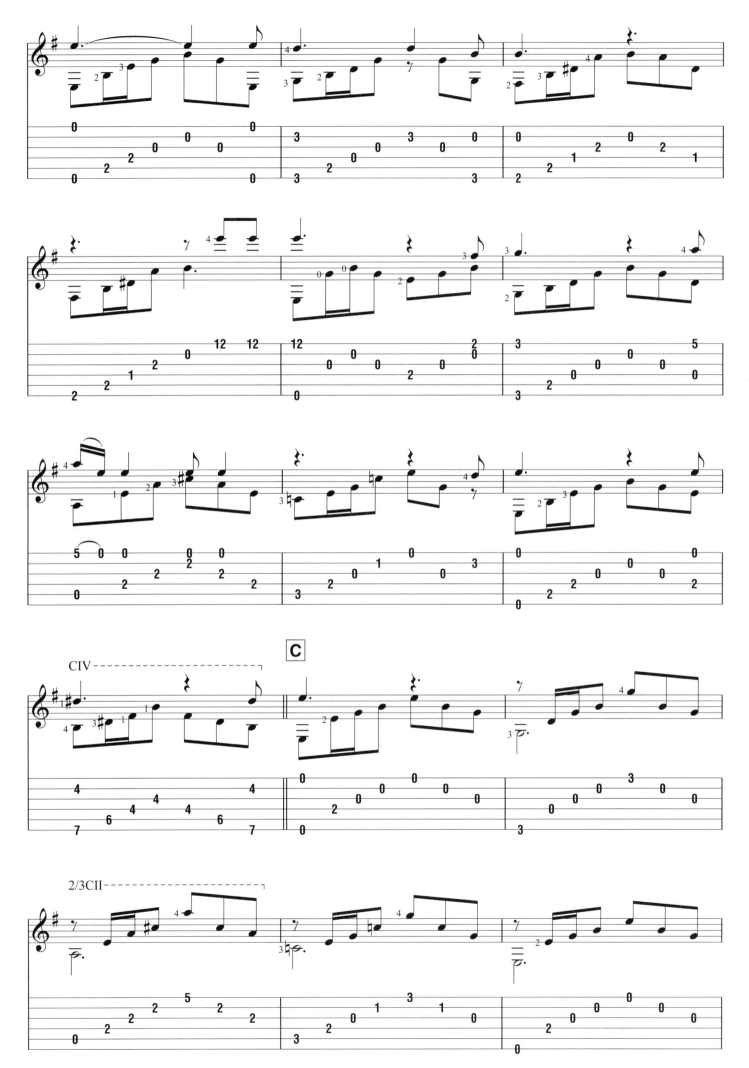

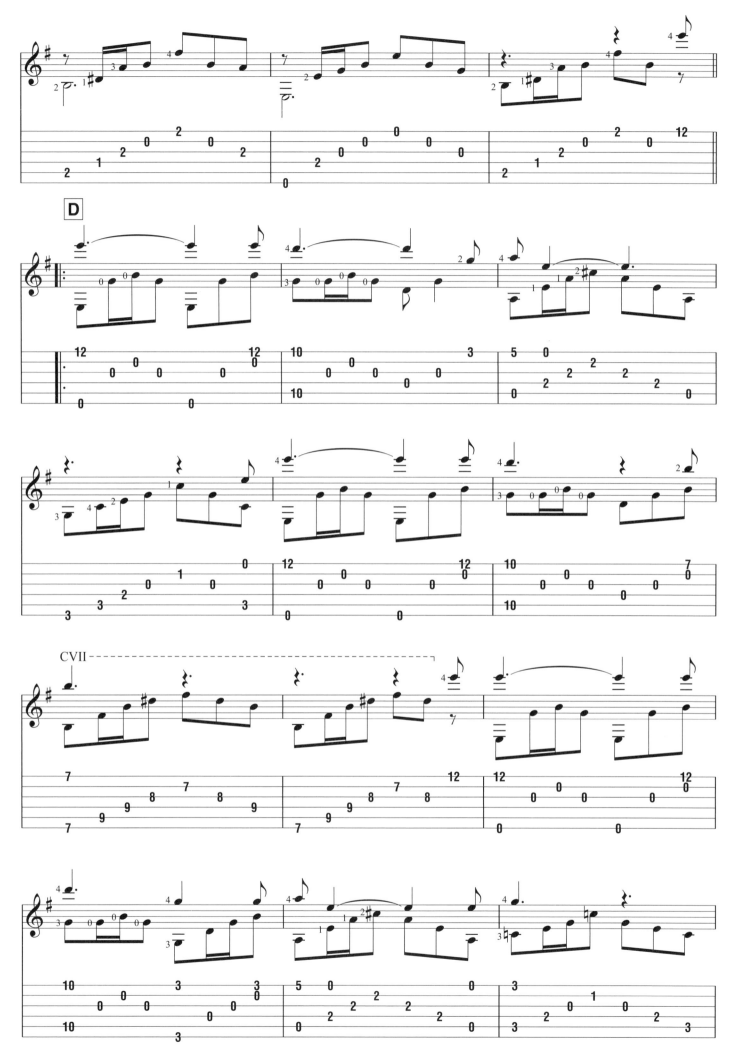

Let It Be

Words and Music by John Lennon and Paul McCartney

Tuning:
(low to high) D-A-D-G-B-E

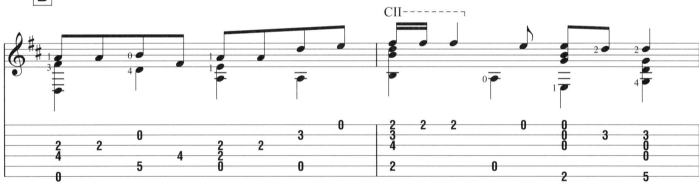

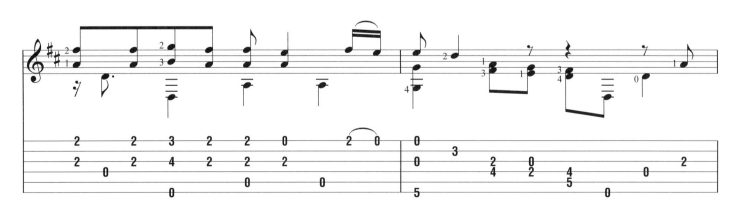

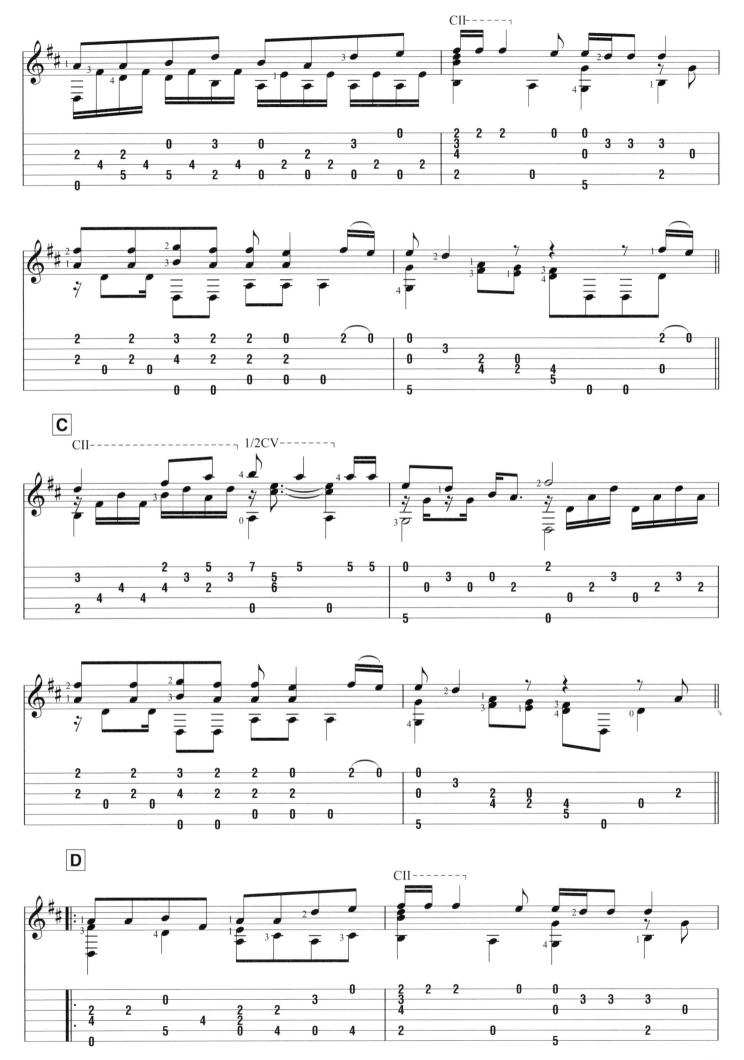

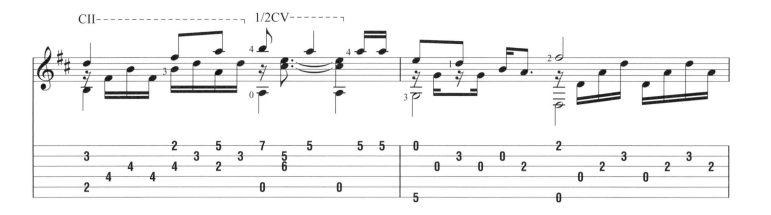

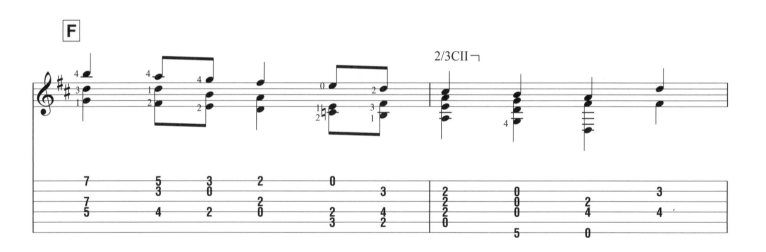

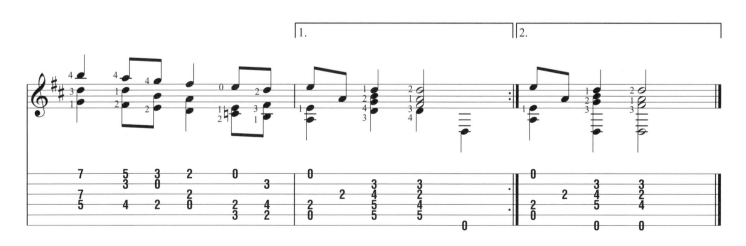

Nights in White Satin

Words and Music by Justin Hayward

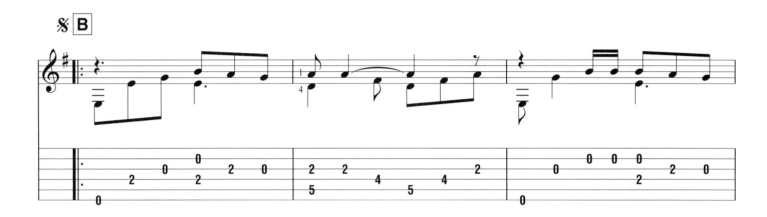

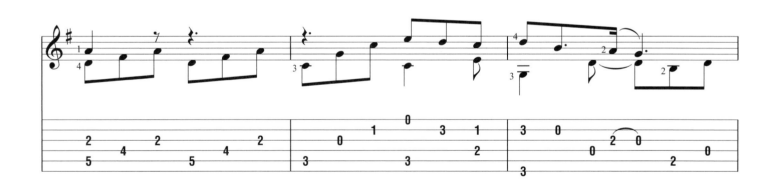

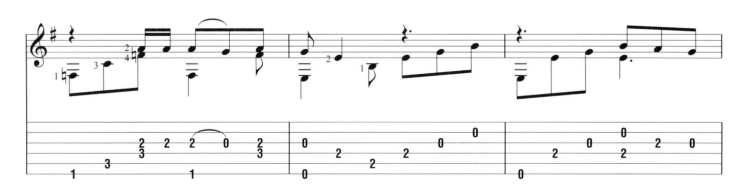

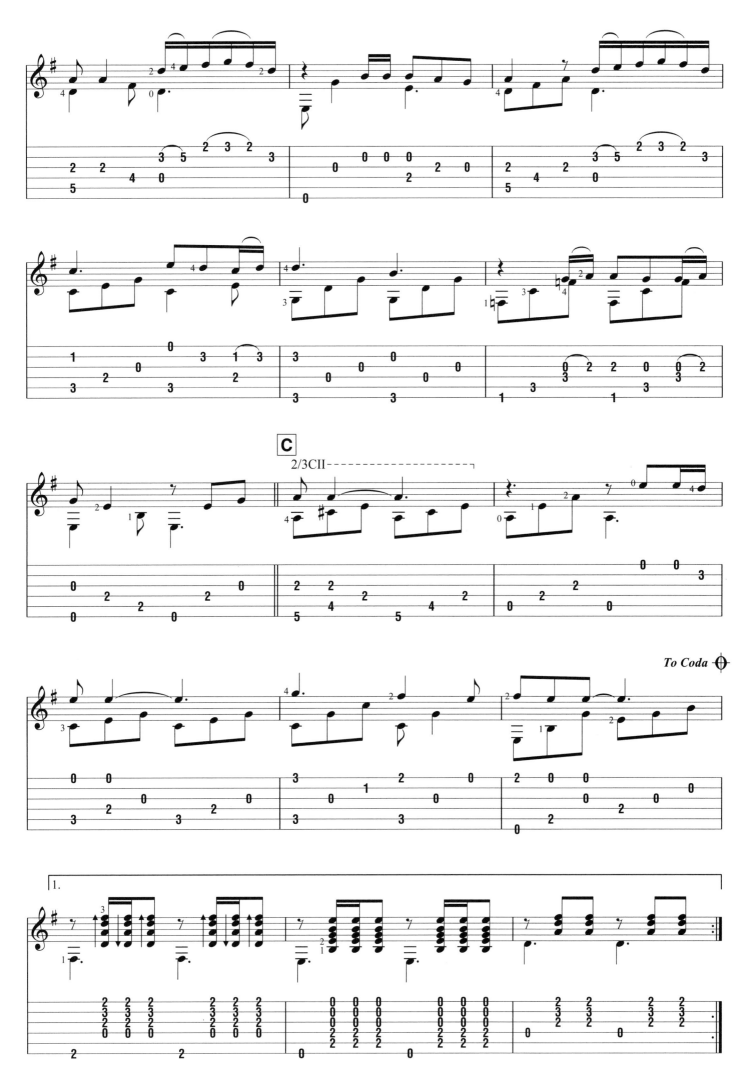

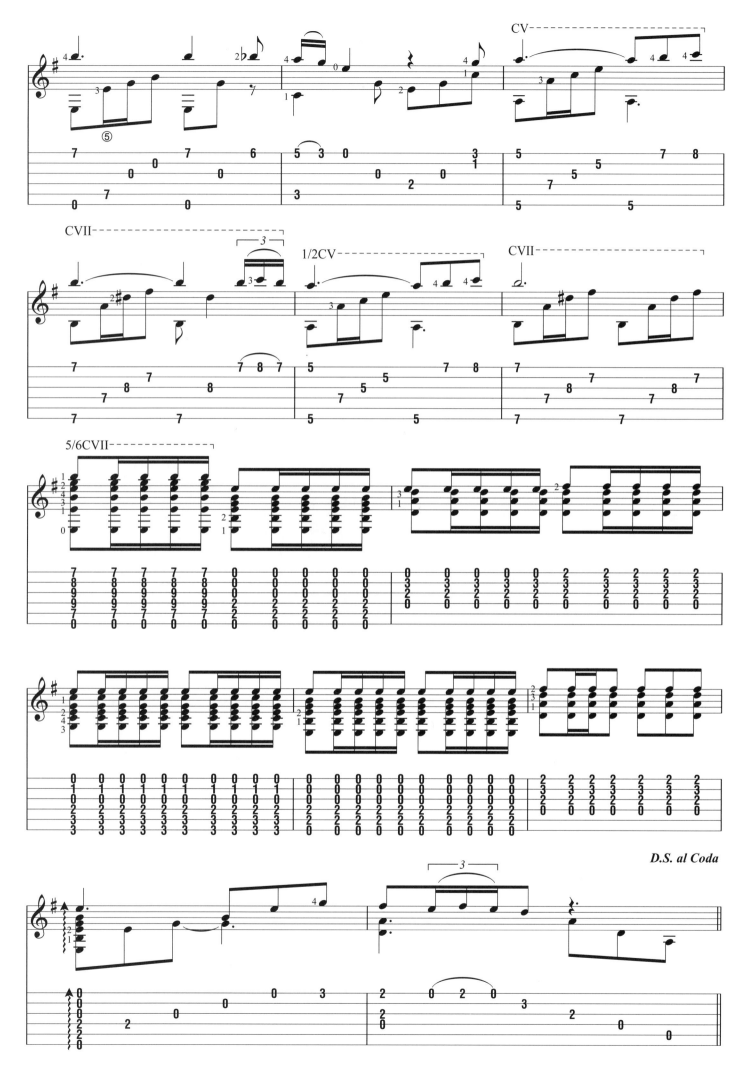

More Than a Feeling

Words and Music by Tom Scholz

Tuning:
(low to high) D-A-D-G-B-E

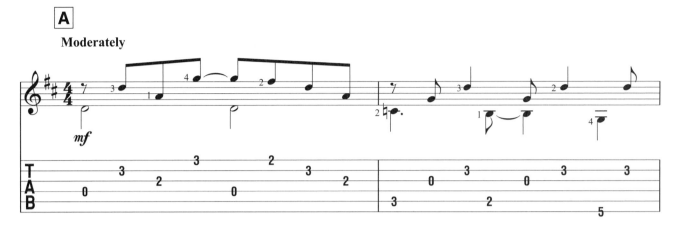

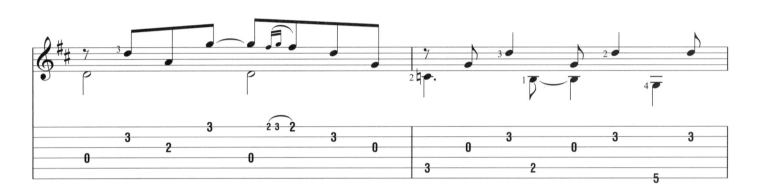

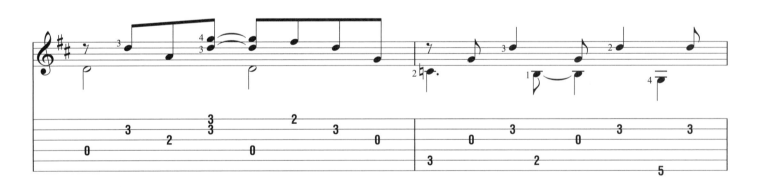

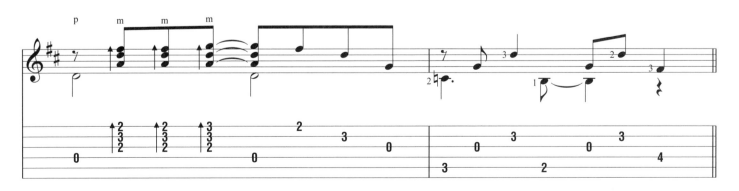

Hotel California

Words and Music by Don Henley, Glenn Frey and Don Felder

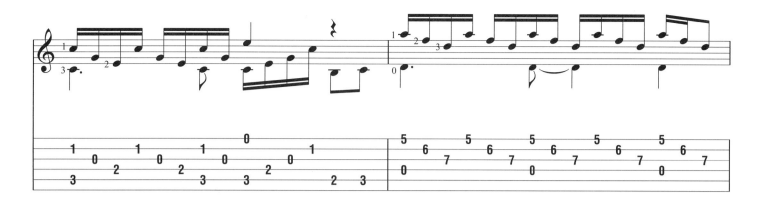

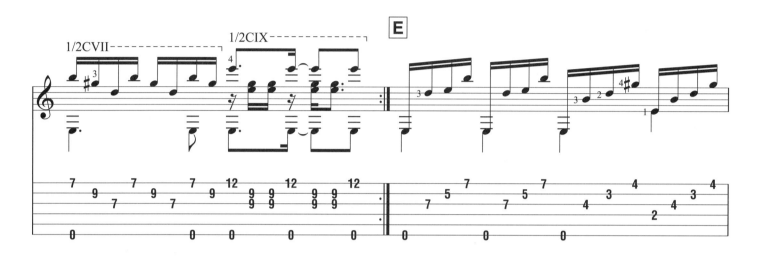

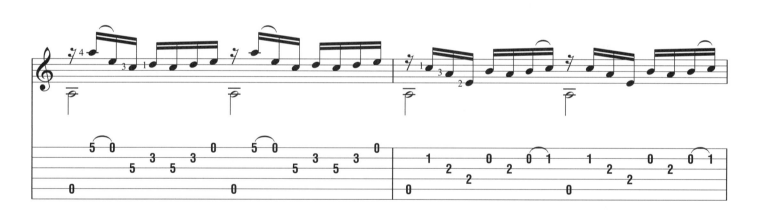

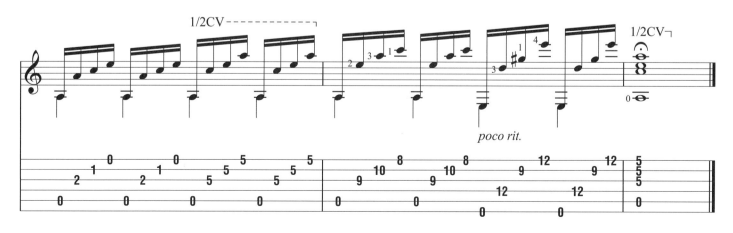

Space Oddity

Words and Music by David Bowie

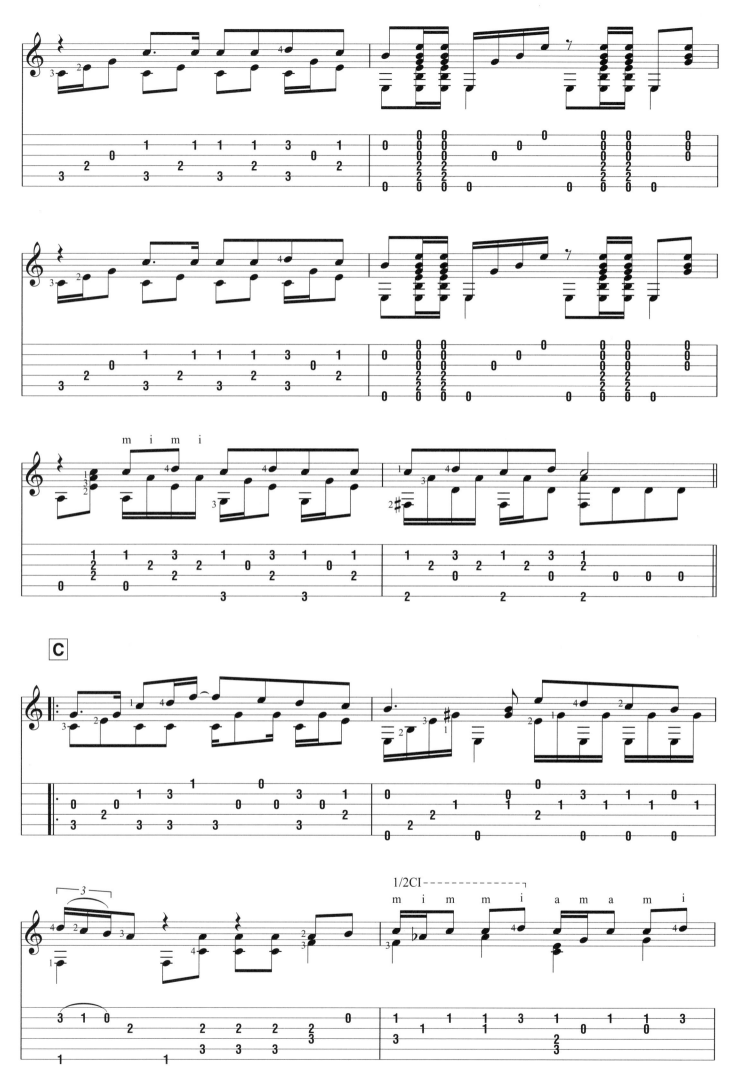

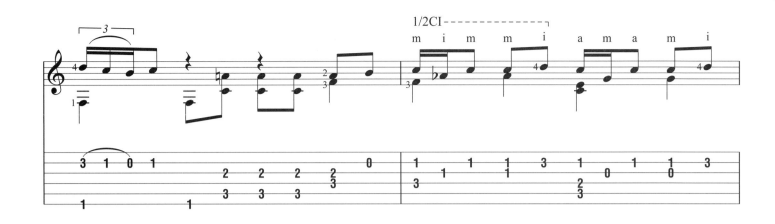

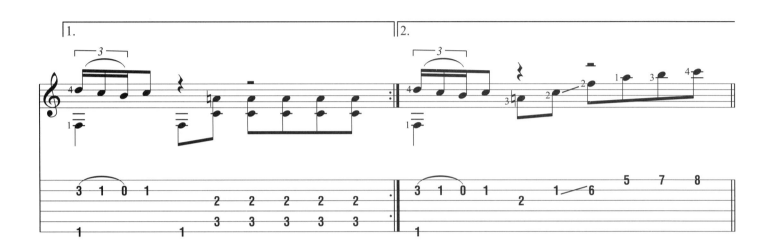

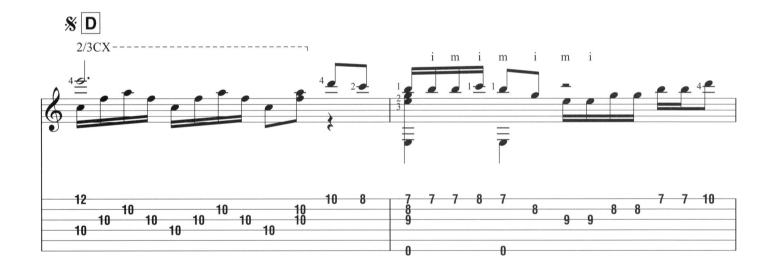

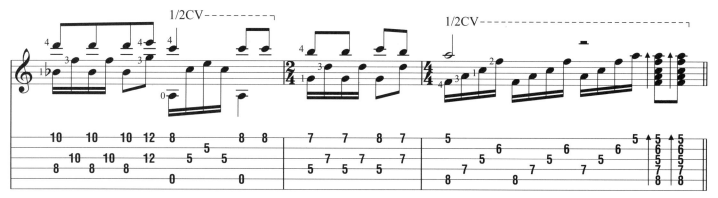

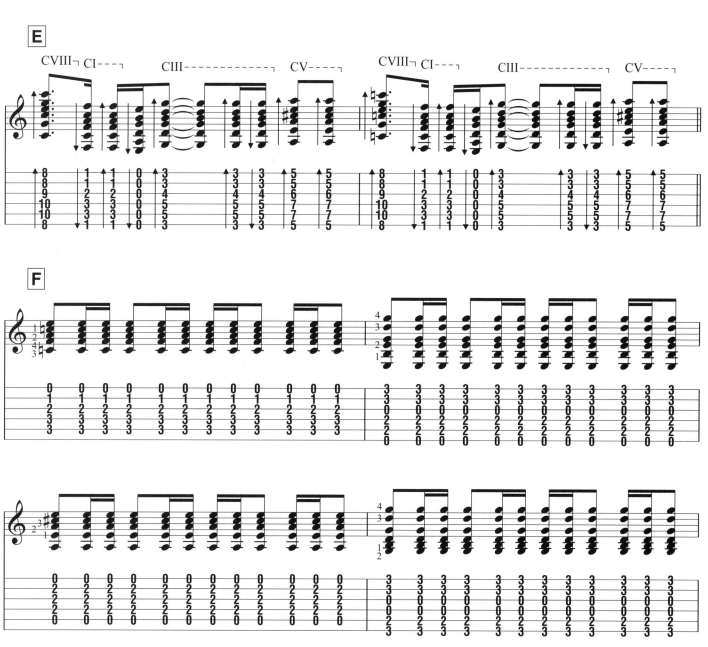

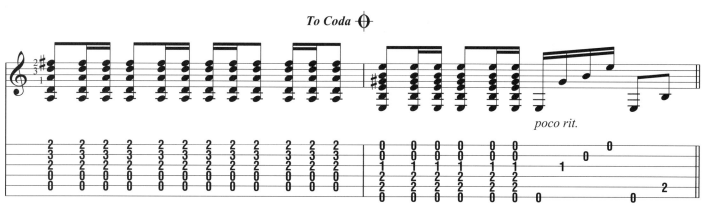

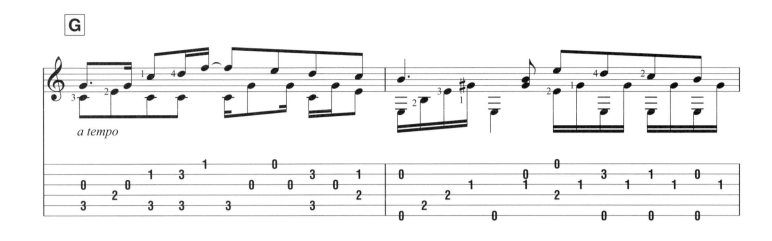

a tempo

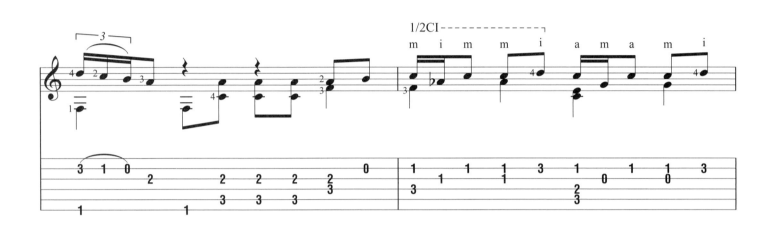

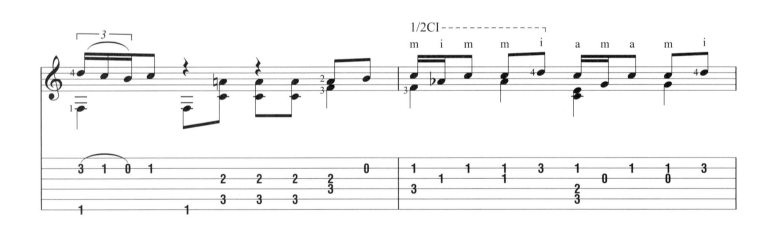

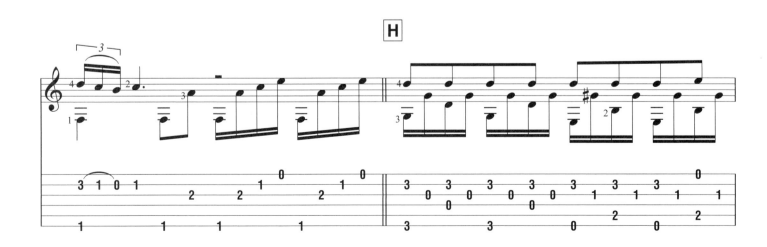

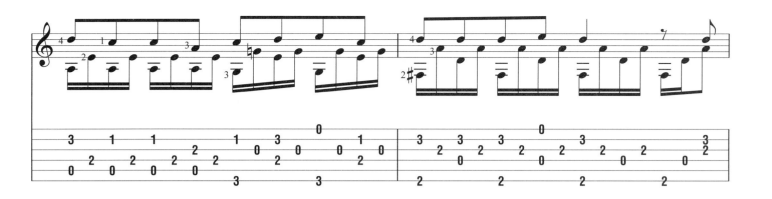

D.S. al Coda

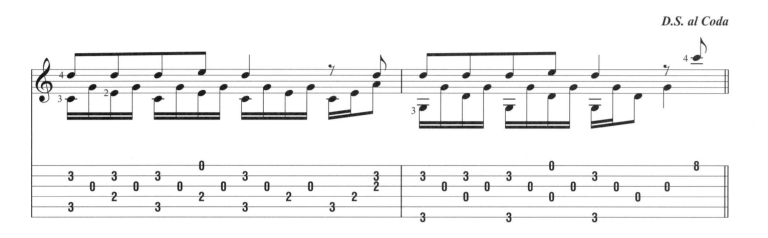

⊕ Coda

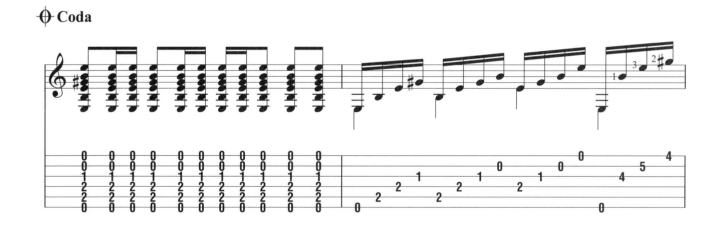

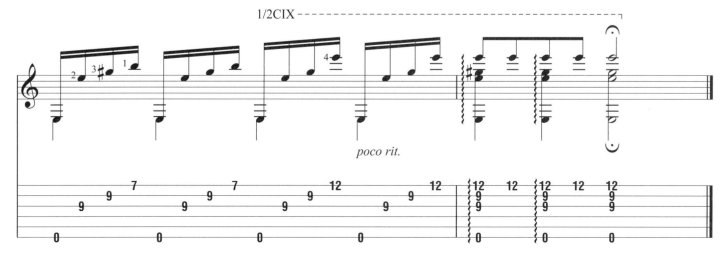

Tears in Heaven

Words and Music by Eric Clapton and Will Jennings

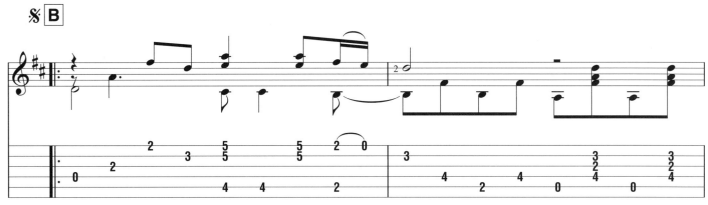

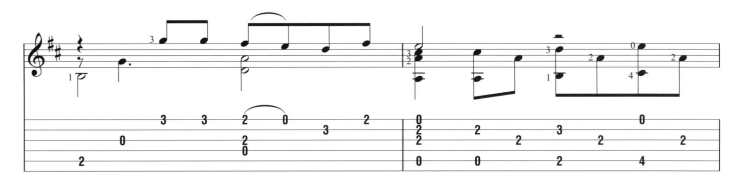

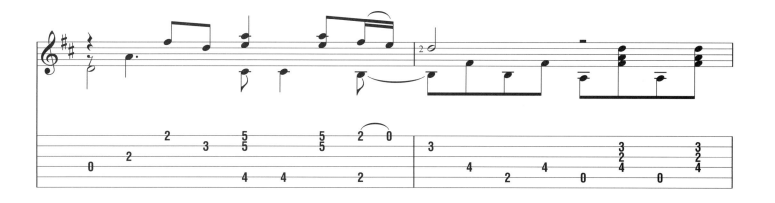

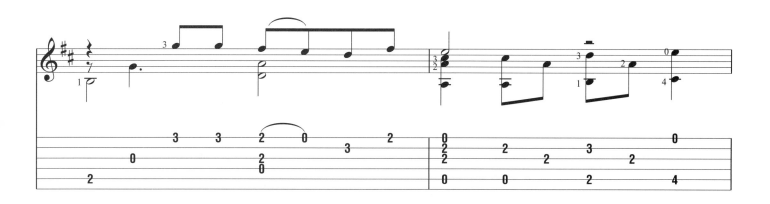

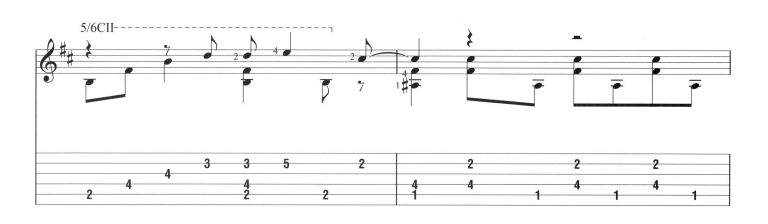

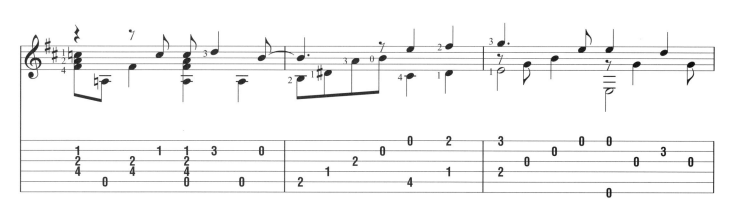

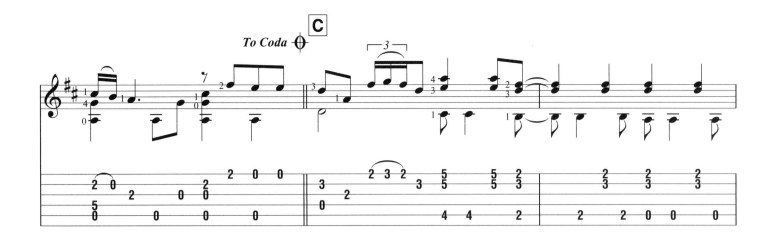

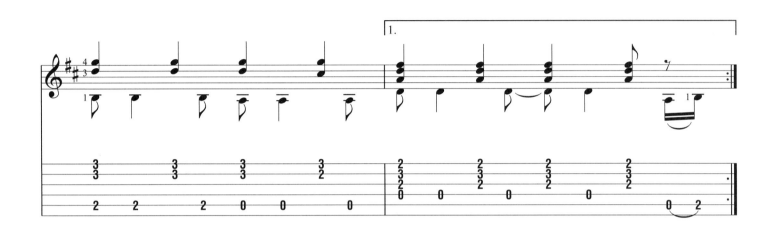

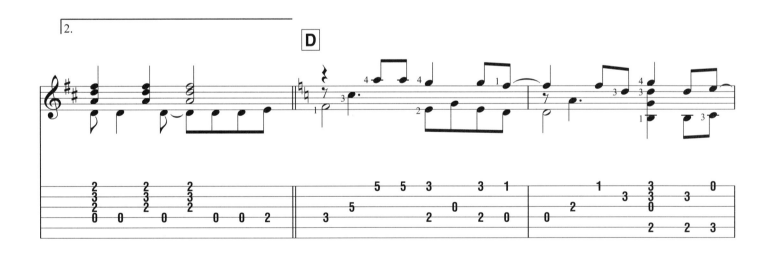

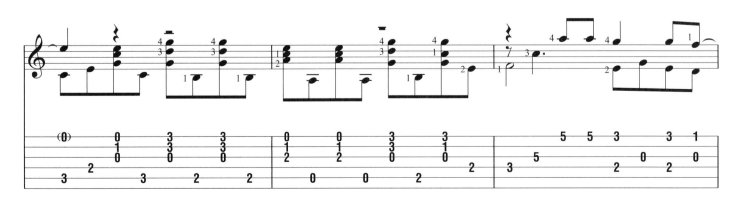

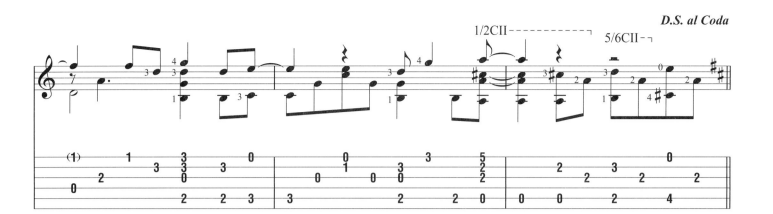

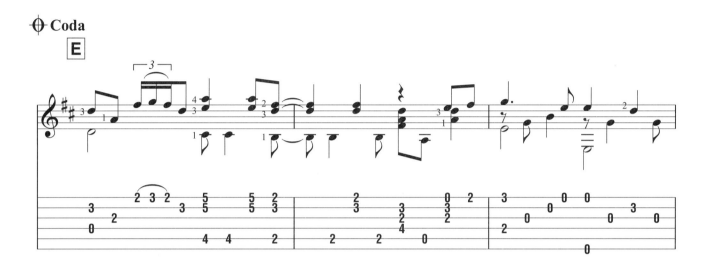

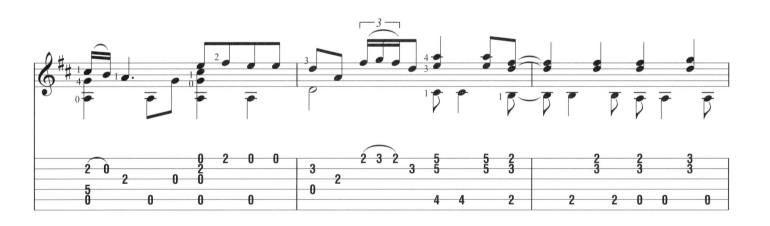

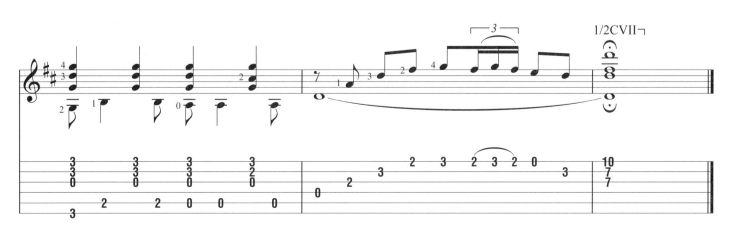

Time in a Bottle

Words and Music by Jim Croce

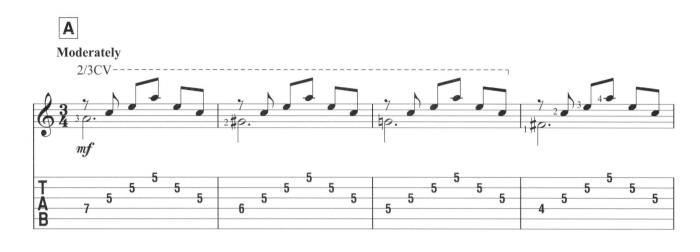

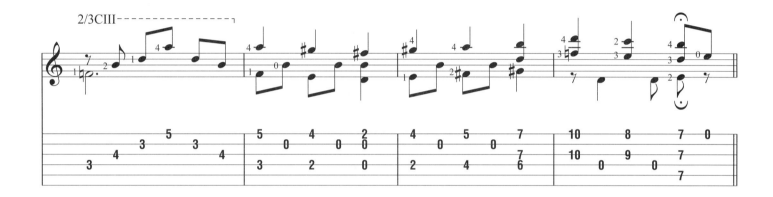

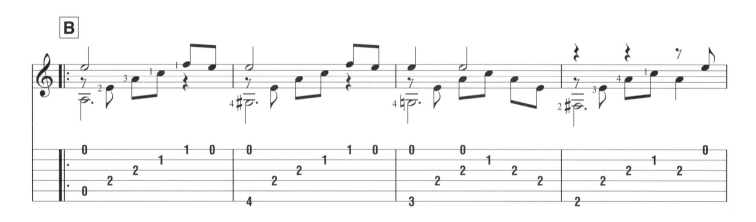

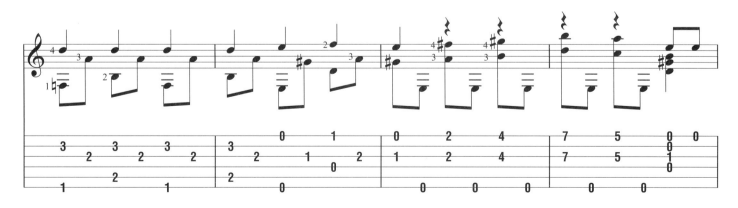

To Coda ⊕

D.C. al Coda
(take 2nd ending)

⊕ **Coda**

Wonderful Tonight

Words and Music by Eric Clapton

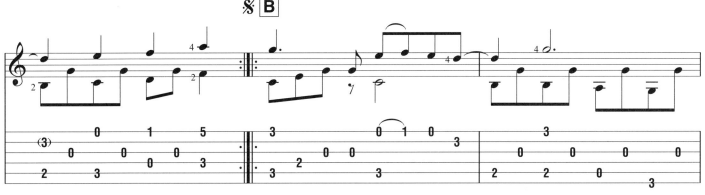

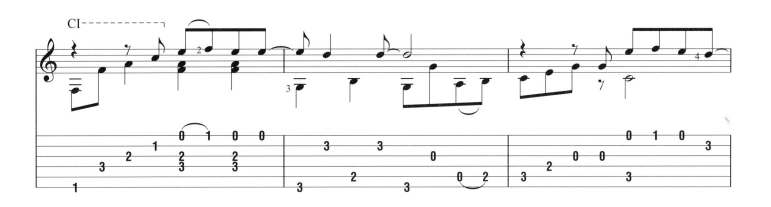

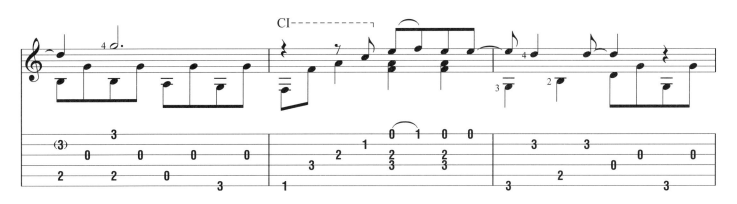

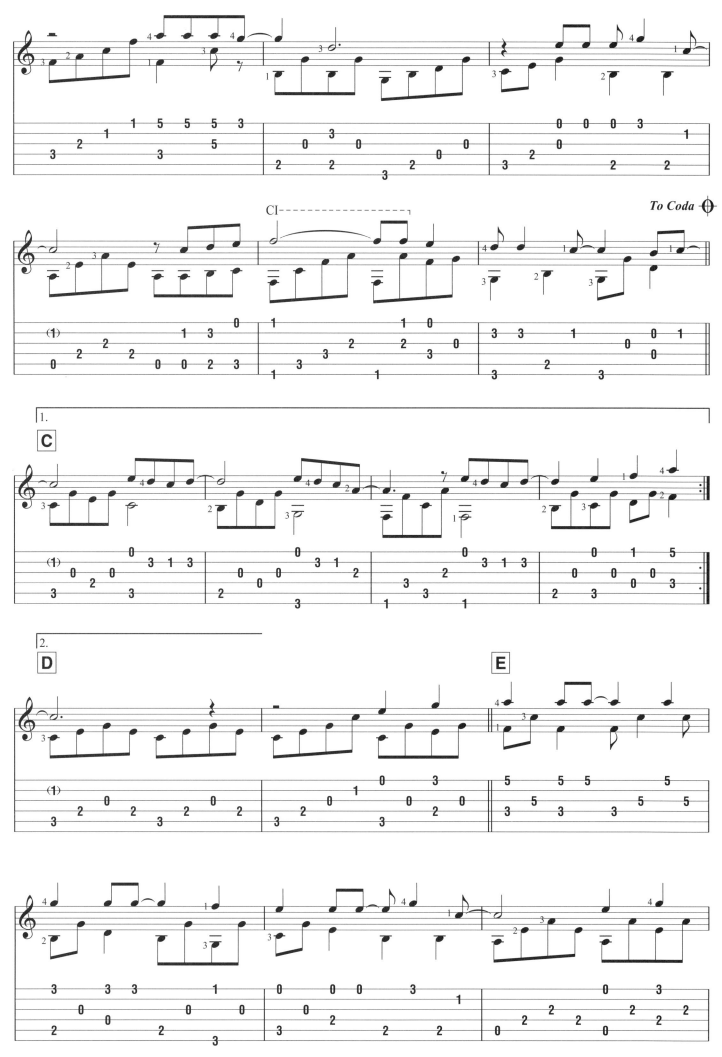

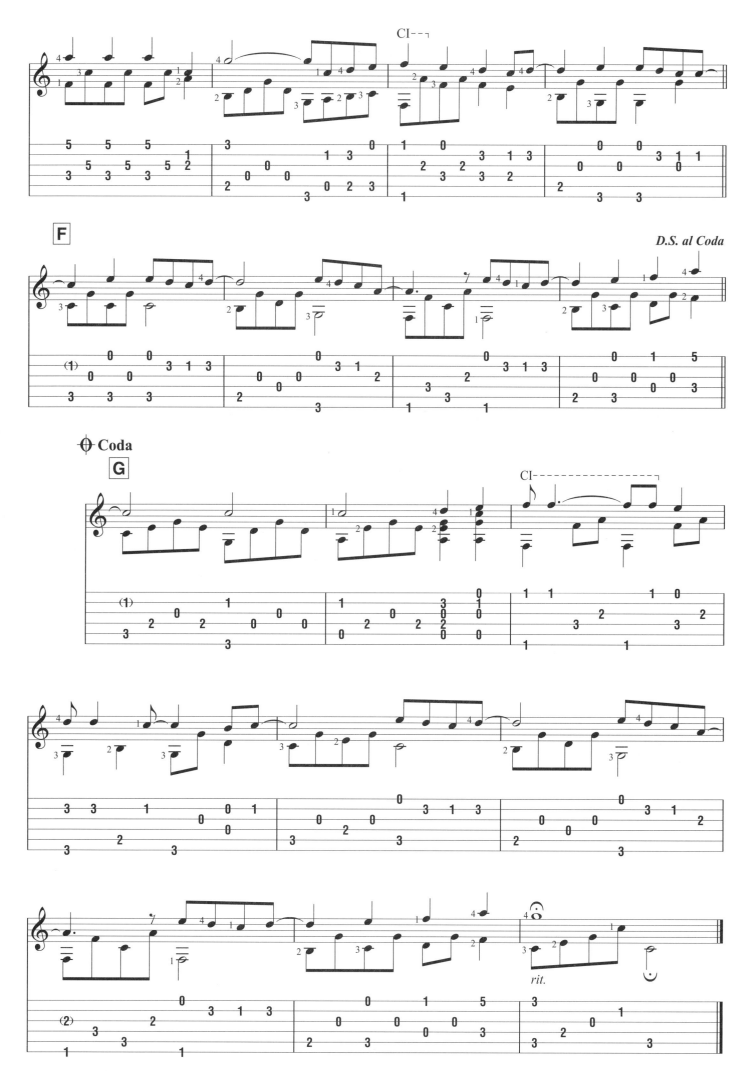

Turn! Turn! Turn!
(To Everything There Is a Season)

Words from the Book of Ecclesiastes
Adaptation and Music by Pete Seeger

Tuning:
(low to high) D-A-D-G-B-E

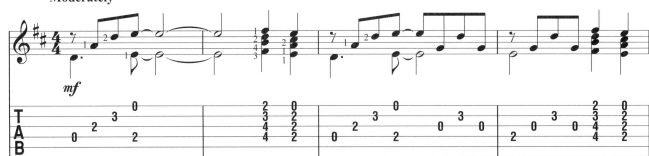

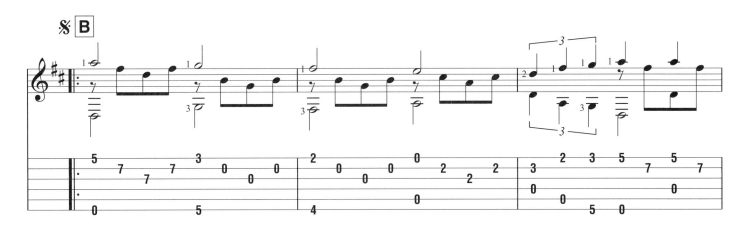

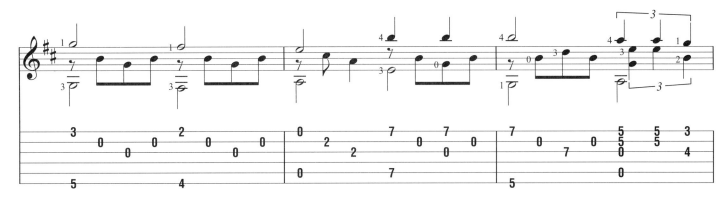

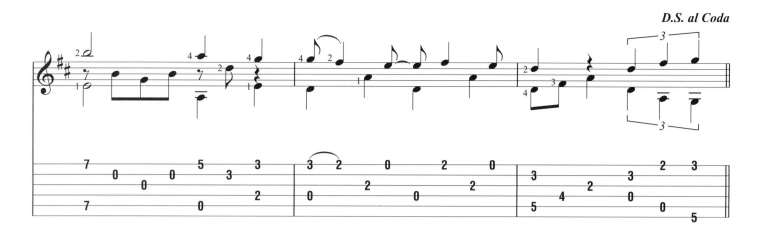

Coda

F

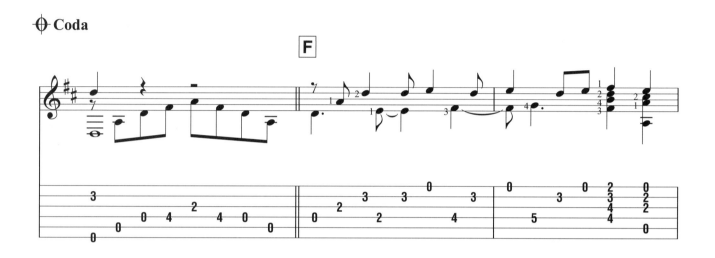

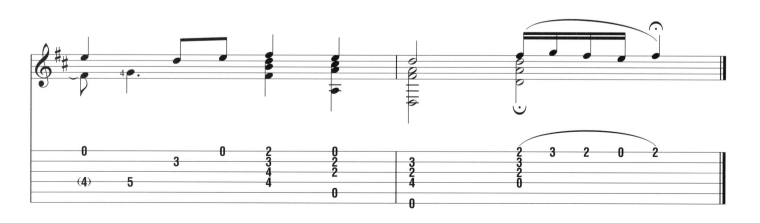

A Whiter Shade of Pale

Words and Music by Keith Reid, Gary Brooker and Matthew Fisher

Tuning:
(low to high) D-A-D-G-B-E

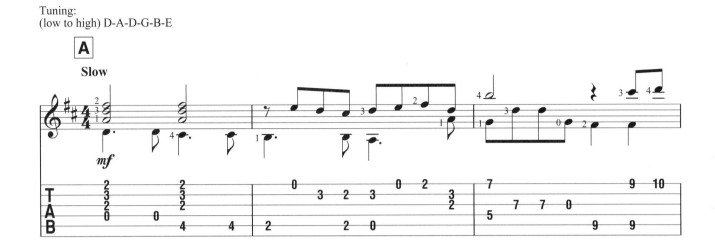

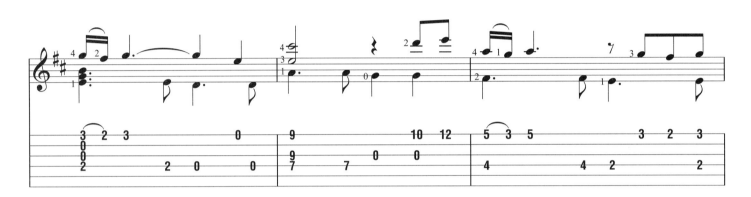

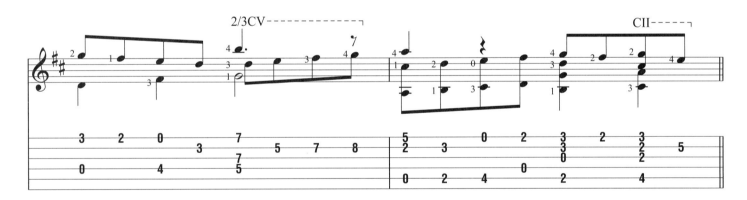

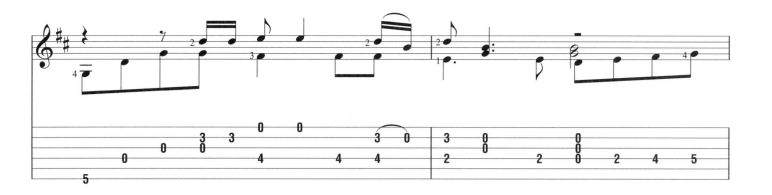

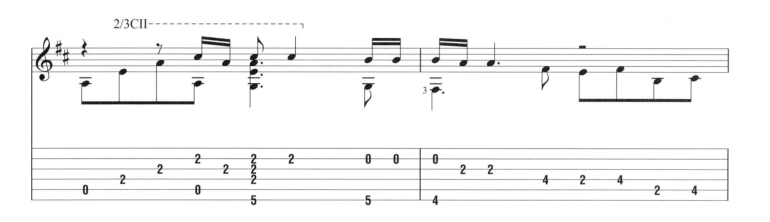

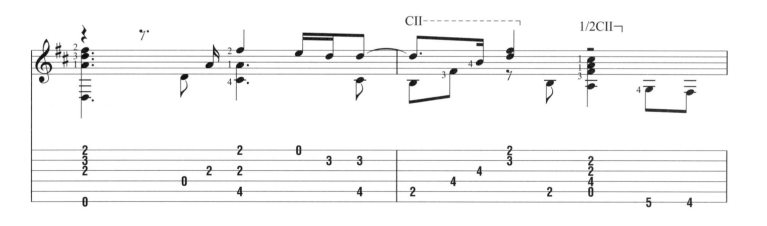

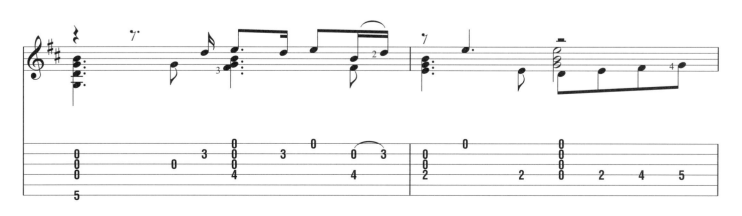

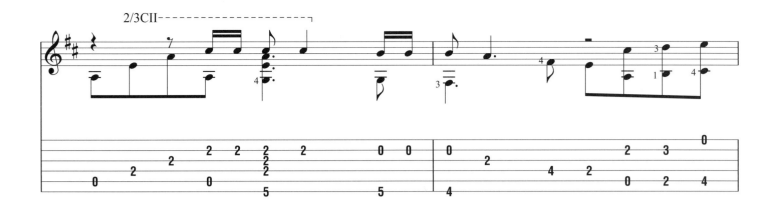

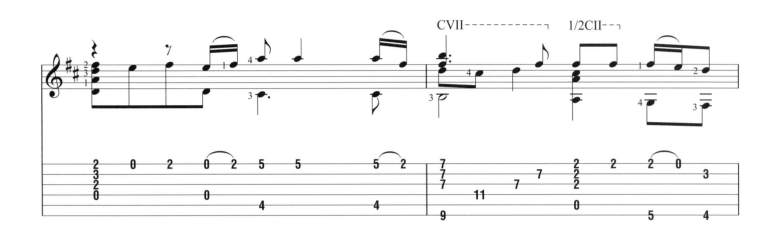

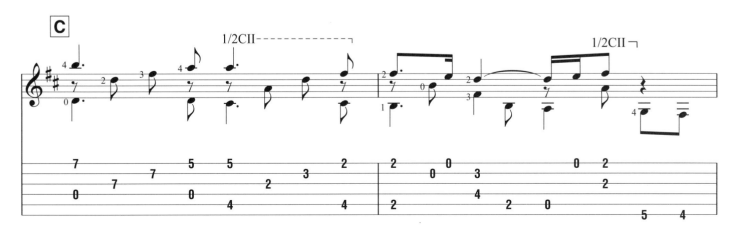

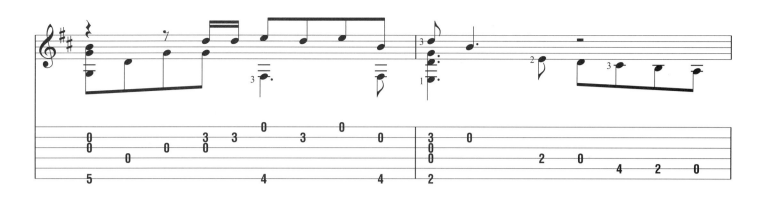

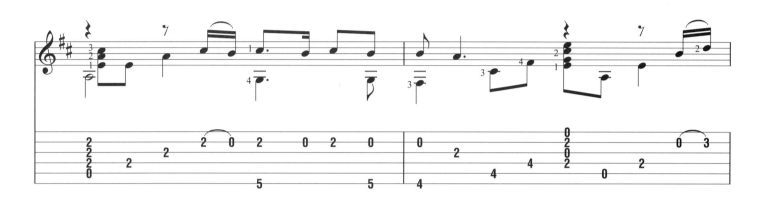

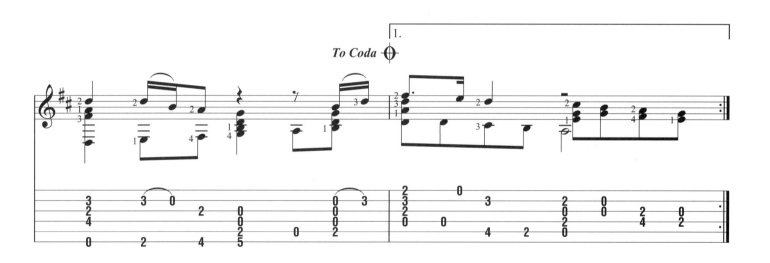

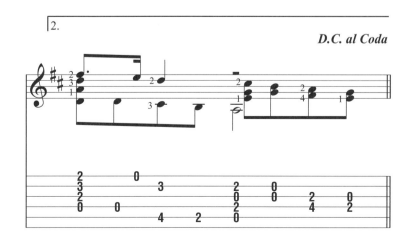

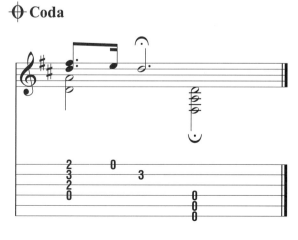

You've Got a Friend

Words and Music by Carole King

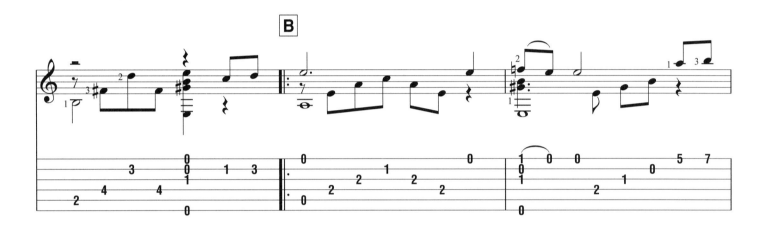

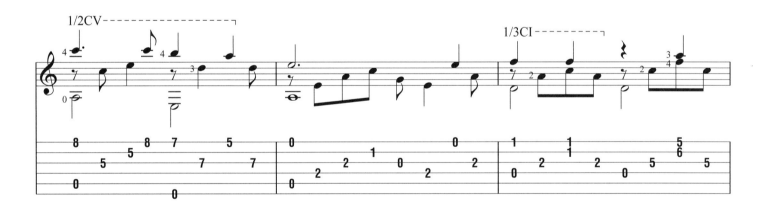

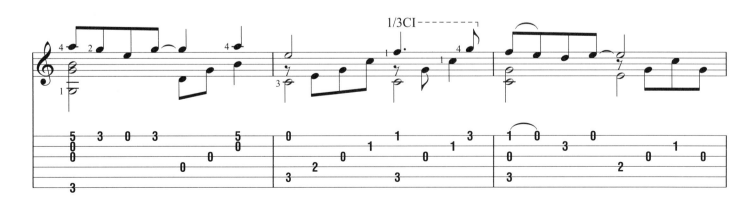

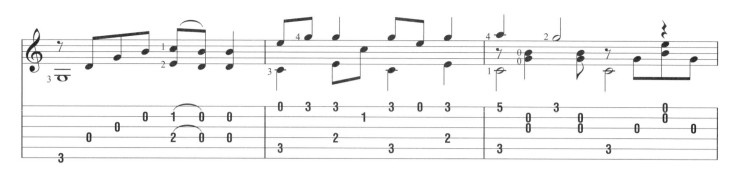

To Coda ✛

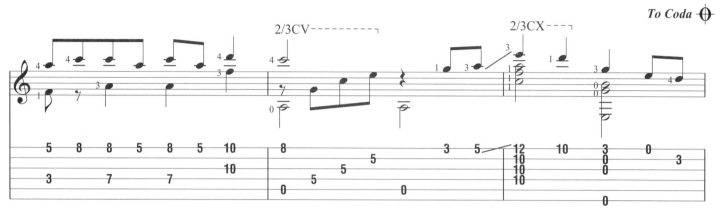

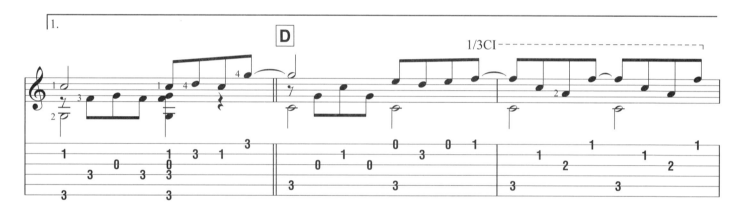

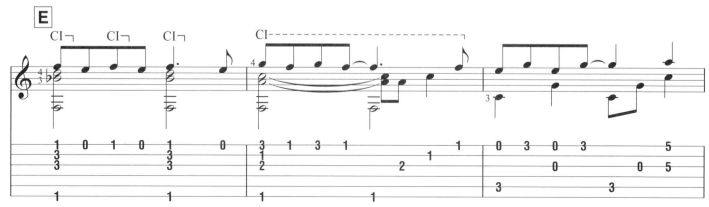

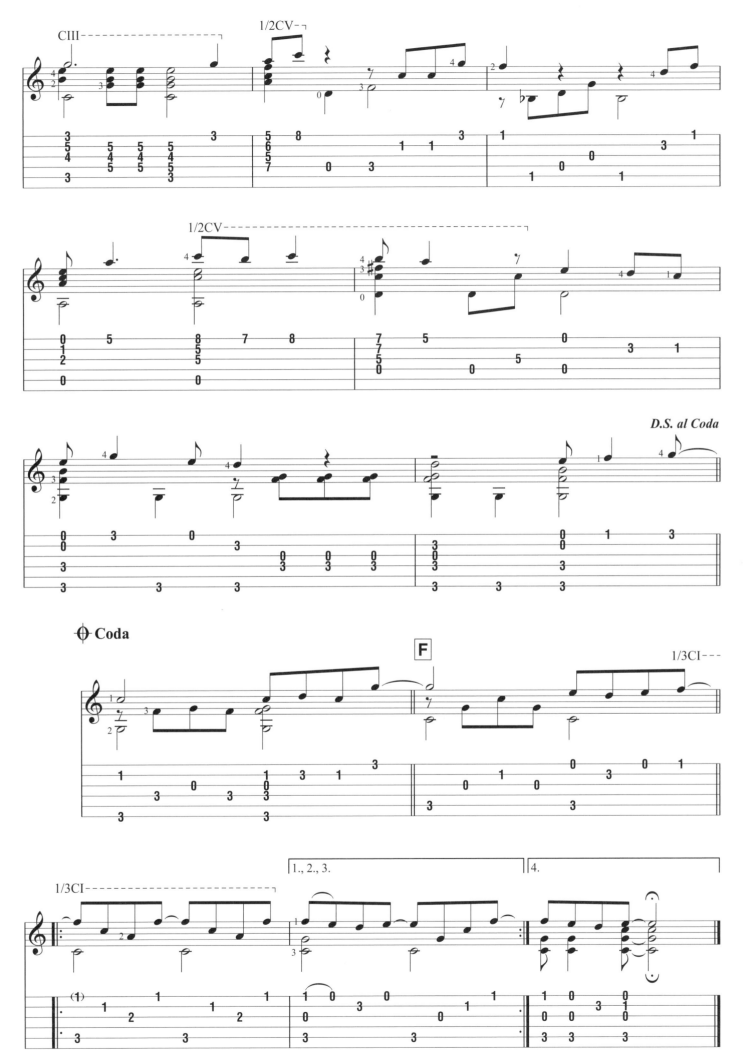

You Are So Beautiful

Words and Music by Billy Preston and Bruce Fisher

Tuning:
(low to high) D-A-D-G-B-E

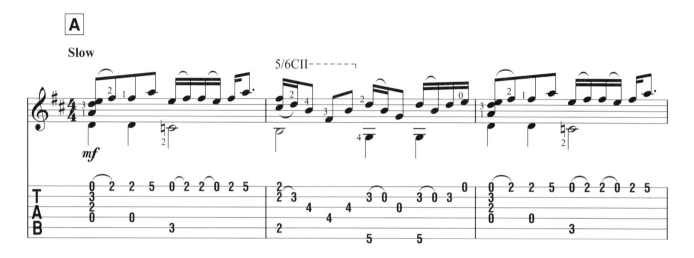

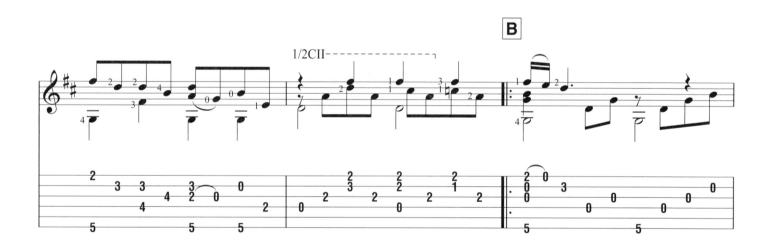

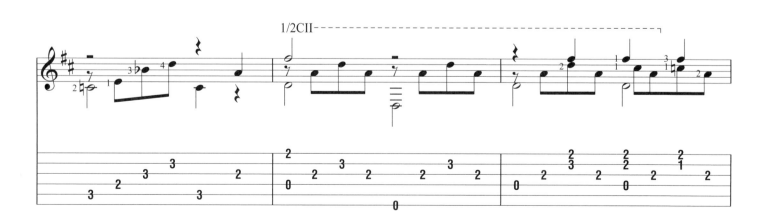

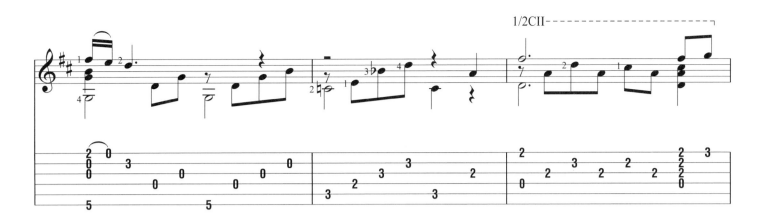

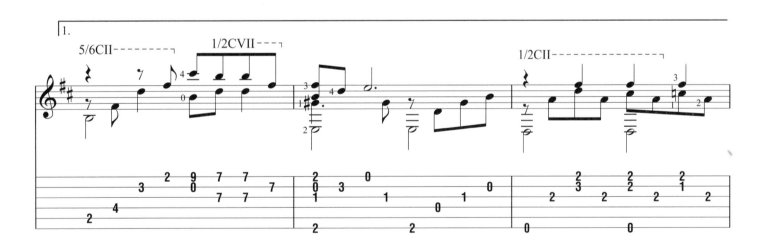

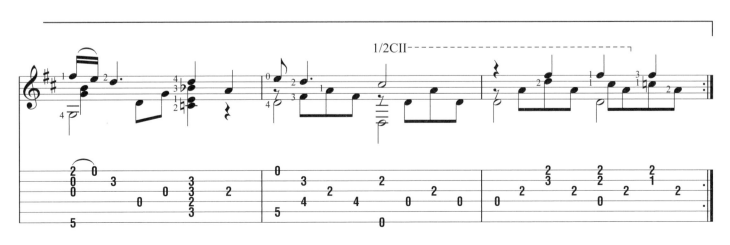

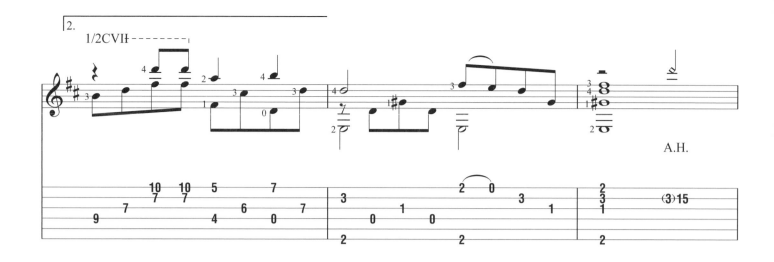

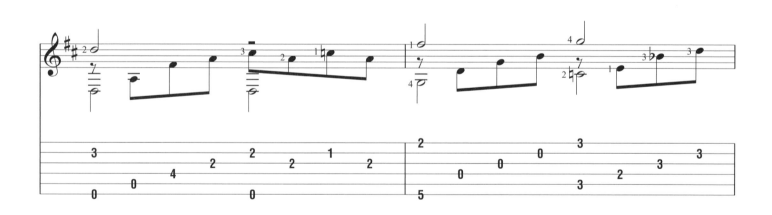

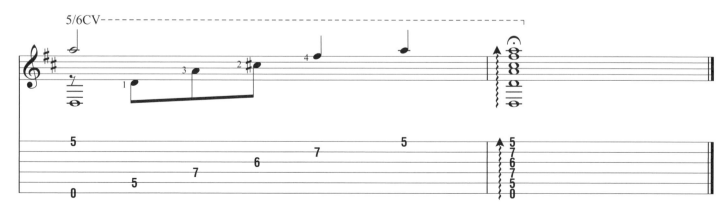

FINGERPICKING GUITAR BOOKS

Hone your fingerpicking skills with these great songbooks featuring solo guitar arrangements in standard notation and tablature. The arrangements in these books are carefully written for intermediate-level guitarists. Each song combines melody and harmony in one superb guitar fingerpicking arrangement. Each book also includes an introduction to basic fingerstyle guitar.

Fingerpicking Acoustic
00699614 15 songs.......................$14.99

Fingerpicking Acoustic Classics
00160211 15 songs.......................$16.99

Fingerpicking Acoustic Hits
00160202 15 songs.......................$12.99

Fingerpicking Acoustic Rock
00699764 14 songs.......................$16.99

Fingerpicking Ballads
00699717 15 songs.......................$15.99

Fingerpicking Beatles
00699049 30 songs.......................$24.99

Fingerpicking Beethoven
00702390 15 pieces.....................$10.99

Fingerpicking Blues
00701277 15 songs $12.99

Fingerpicking Broadway Favorites
00699843 15 songs.......................$9.99

Fingerpicking Broadway Hits
00699838 15 songs.......................$7.99

Fingerpicking Campfire
00275964 15 songs.......................$14.99

Fingerpicking Celtic Folk
00701148 15 songs.......................$12.99

Fingerpicking Children's Songs
00699712 15 songs.......................$9.99

Fingerpicking Christian
00701076 15 songs.......................$12.99

Fingerpicking Christmas
00699599 20 carols.....................$12.99

Fingerpicking Christmas Classics
00701695 15 songs.......................$7.99

Fingerpicking Christmas Songs
00171333 15 songs.......................$10.99

Fingerpicking Classical
00699620 15 pieces.....................$10.99

Fingerpicking Country
00699687 17 songs.......................$12.99

Fingerpicking Disney
00699711 15 songs.......................$17.99

Fingerpicking Early Jazz Standards
00276565 15 songs $12.99

Fingerpicking Duke Ellington
00699845 15 songs.......................$9.99

Fingerpicking Enya
00701161 15 songs.......................$16.99

Fingerpicking Film Score Music
00160143 15 songs.......................$12.99

Fingerpicking Gospel
00701059 15 songs.......................$9.99

Fingerpicking Hit Songs
00160195 15 songs.......................$12.99

Fingerpicking Hymns
00699688 15 hymns $12.99

Fingerpicking Irish Songs
00701965 15 songs.......................$10.99

Fingerpicking Italian Songs
00159778 15 songs.......................$12.99

Fingerpicking Jazz Favorites
00699844 15 songs.......................$12.99

Fingerpicking Jazz Standards
00699840 15 songs.......................$12.99

Fingerpicking Elton John
00237495 15 songs.......................$15.99

Fingerpicking Latin Favorites
00699842 15 songs.......................$12.99

Fingerpicking Latin Standards
00699837 15 songs.......................$17.99

Fingerpicking Andrew Lloyd Webber
00699839 14 songs.......................$16.99

Fingerpicking Love Songs
00699841 15 songs.......................$14.99

Fingerpicking Love Standards
00699836 15 songs.......................$9.99

Fingerpicking Lullabyes
00701276 16 songs.......................$9.99

Fingerpicking Movie Music
00699919 15 songs.......................$14.99

Fingerpicking Mozart
00699794 15 pieces.....................$10.99

Fingerpicking Pop
00699615 15 songs.......................$14.99

Fingerpicking Popular Hits
00139079 14 songs.......................$12.99

Fingerpicking Praise
00699714 15 songs.......................$14.99

Fingerpicking Rock
00699716 15 songs.......................$14.99

Fingerpicking Standards
00699613 17 songs.......................$15.99

Fingerpicking Wedding
00699637 15 songs.......................$10.99

Fingerpicking Worship
00700554 15 songs.......................$14.99

Fingerpicking Neil Young – Greatest Hits
00700134 16 songs.......................$17.99

Fingerpicking Yuletide
00699654 16 songs.......................$12.99

HAL•LEONARD®

Order these and more great publications from your favorite music retailer at
halleonard.com

Prices, contents and availability subject to change without notice.

    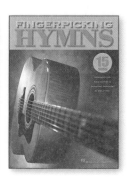 

JAZZ GUITAR CHORD MELODY SOLOS

This series features chord melody arrangements in standard notation and tablature of songs for intermediate guitarists.

INCLUDES TAB

ALL-TIME STANDARDS

27 songs, including: All of Me • Bewitched • Come Fly with Me • A Fine Romance • Georgia on My Mind • How High the Moon • I'll Never Smile Again • I've Got You Under My Skin • It's De-Lovely • It's Only a Paper Moon • My Romance • Satin Doll • The Surrey with the Fringe on Top • Yesterdays • and more.
00699757 Solo Guitar...........................$16.99

IRVING BERLIN

27 songs, including: Alexander's Ragtime Band • Always • Blue Skies • Cheek to Cheek • Easter Parade • Happy Holiday • Heat Wave • How Deep Is the Ocean • Puttin' On the Ritz • Remember • They Say It's Wonderful • What'll I Do? • White Christmas • and more.
00700637 Solo Guitar...........................$14.99

CHRISTMAS CAROLS

26 songs, including: Auld Lang Syne • Away in a Manger • Deck the Hall • God Rest Ye Merry, Gentlemen • Good King Wenceslas • Here We Come A-Wassailing • It Came upon the Midnight Clear • Joy to the World • O Holy Night • O Little Town of Bethlehem • Silent Night • Toyland • We Three Kings of Orient Are • and more.
00701697 Solo Guitar $14.99

CHRISTMAS JAZZ

21 songs, including Auld Lang Syne • Baby, It's Cold Outside • Cool Yule • Have Yourself a Merry Little Christmas • I've Got My Love to Keep Me Warm • Mary, Did You Know? • Santa Baby • Sleigh Ride • White Christmas • Winter Wonderland • and more.
00171334 Solo Guitar...........................$15.99

DISNEY SONGS

27 songs, including: Beauty and the Beast • Can You Feel the Love Tonight • Candle on the Water • Colors of the Wind • A Dream Is a Wish Your Heart Makes • Heigh-Ho • Some Day My Prince Will Come • Under the Sea • When You Wish upon a Star • A Whole New World (Aladdin's Theme) • Zip-A-Dee-Doo-Dah • and more.
00701902 Solo Guitar $14.99

DUKE ELLINGTON

25 songs, including: C-Jam Blues • Caravan • Do Nothin' Till You Hear from Me • Don't Get Around Much Anymore • I Got It Bad and That Ain't Good • I'm Just a Lucky So and So • In a Sentimental Mood • It Don't Mean a Thing (If It Ain't Got That Swing) • Mood Indigo • Perdido • Prelude to a Kiss • Satin Doll • and more.
00700636 Solo Guitar $14.99

FAVORITE STANDARDS

27 songs, including: All the Way • Autumn in New York • Blue Skies • Cheek to Cheek • Don't Get Around Much Anymore • How Deep Is the Ocean • I'll Be Seeing You • Isn't It Romantic? • It Could Happen to You • The Lady Is a Tramp • Moon River • Speak Low • Take the "A" Train • Willow Weep for Me • Witchcraft • and more.
00699756 Solo Guitar...........................$17.99

JAZZ BALLADS

27 songs, including: Body and Soul • Darn That Dream • Easy to Love (You'd Be So Easy to Love) • Here's That Rainy Day • In a Sentimental Mood • Misty • My Foolish Heart • My Funny Valentine • The Nearness of You • Stella by Starlight • Time After Time • The Way You Look Tonight • When Sunny Gets Blue • and more.
00699755 Solo Guitar...........................$16.99

LATIN STANDARDS

27 Latin favorites, including: Água De Beber (Water to Drink) • Desafinado • The Girl from Ipanema • How Insensitive (Insensatez) • Little Boat • Meditation • One Note Samba (Samba De Uma Nota So) • Poinciana • Quiet Nights of Quiet Stars • Samba De Orfeu • So Nice (Summer Samba) • Wave • and more.
00699754 Solo Guitar...........................$16.99

Order online at **halleonard.com**

HAL•LEONARD®